The House of Tudor

An Enthralling Overview of the History of the Tudors

Free limited time bonus

Stop for a moment. We have a free bonus set up for you. The problem is this: we forget 90% of everything that we read after 7 days. Crazy fact, right? Here's the solution: we've created a printable, 1-page pdf summary for this book that you're reading now. All you have to do to get your free pdf summary is to go to the following website: **https://livetolearn.lpages.co/enthrallinghistory/**

Once you do, it will be intuitive. Enjoy, and thank you!

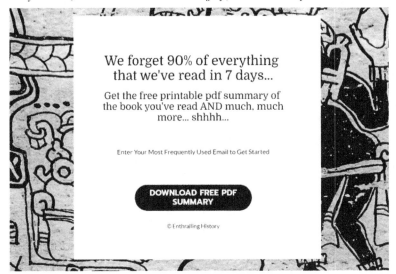

We forget 90% of everything that we've read in 7 days...

Get the free printable pdf summary of the book you've read AND much, much more... shhhh...

Enter Your Most Frequently Used Email to Get Started

DOWNLOAD FREE PDF SUMMARY

© Enthralling History

Contents

Introduction

The House of Tudor is arguably England's most famous ruling dynasty. In the wake of the Wars of the Roses, the country was divided and war-torn since its leaders had been fighting against each other for control. For decades, the most prominent families in England vied for the throne and found themselves split between the House of York and the House of Lancaster. The mighty Plantagenet dynasty had come to a nasty end, and someone needed to take control. With legitimate heirs to the throne on both sides of the war, England was ravaged by ambitious and powerful individuals.

Finally, at the Battle of Bosworth Field, a victor emerged and claimed his crown on the battlefield. Henry Tudor became Henry VII, and England would never be the same again. Along with his tight-knit council, he ruled England and navigated his country through the aftermath of one of the bloodiest civil wars in its history. While Henry's rule ushered in a new period of peace, his dynasty became the center of intrigue and political plotting that lasted for generations until the Tudor line ended with his granddaughter, Elizabeth I.

This comprehensive guide to the fascinating Tudor family discusses the origins of the royal house, whose roots were founded in Wales and France. The first part of the book delves into what events led to Henry VII being crowned on the battlefield. It will explore interesting topics such as the fall of the Plantagenet dynasty and the origin of the Tudor line. After establishing the foundation of the House of Tudor, an explanation of the Tudors' rise to power will be provided.

Once the Tudors secured the throne, four more Tudors would take the throne in less than fifty years, with the family line ending with Elizabeth I. The second part of the book is dedicated to discovering more about the Tudor rulers. Each chapter outlines the lives and influences of those monarchs. The Tudor family was deeply divided, and each member of the family had their own agenda. Henry VII had two male heirs, but when his firstborn son, Arthur, died, a new heir had to be primed for the throne. Henry VIII wasn't born to be king, but he found himself as the heir to the English throne when he was only a boy. He was trained under his father and received the best education in the world, but by the end of his reign, he was seen as a tyrant with a murderous reputation. While three of the Tudor monarchs were siblings, they had wildly different policies and ideals.

The Tudor dynasty was built on war and sacrifice, which means that Tudor history features some of the most famous English battles. Starting with the Wars of the Roses and ending with "Elizabeth Gloriana," the third part of the book will discuss the battles that helped to define the Tudor line. Besides discussing famous battles, there are chapters dedicated to discussing the Tudors' military and weapons that helped them win vital battles, as well as the failures that contributed to some catastrophic losses.

Finally, life during the Tudor dynasty wasn't always easy. Henry VII inherited a throne that was weakened by wars and a treasury that reflected the devastation of those wars. Henry VIII was a changeable king who led his people through religious and political turmoil, most of which he personally caused. His children were religiously divided, and his male heir was little more than a child who was used to promoting the ideals of his advisors. When he died, his half-sister, Mary I, seized the throne and decided to reform the country. She earned the title "Bloody Mary" and caused more religious turmoil. Finally, Elizabeth I took the throne, and while she was a more popular leader, her rule wasn't always peaceful. While the Tudor monarchs and their courts are a continuous source of fascination, the common people were intensely impacted by the whims of these monarchs. The final section of this book reveals what life was like for the subjects of the Tudor dynasty and discusses social factors such as religion, education, and art.

The Tudor dynasty was marked by some of the most significant periods in English history, and this book organizes those events in a simple format. It features accurate information that explains the religious, political, and social factors that made the House of Tudor unique. Discover personal profiles about some of the most famous rulers in history, and get to know the dynamic individuals who built and ended the Tudor dynasty.

The Tudors were one of the most intriguing ruling families in history, and this book brings their struggles and triumphs to life.

Part One: England before the House of Tudor

Chapter 1: England before the Tudors

The Tudor family had a lasting effect on English history and ushered in a new era. However, before they came to the throne, Britain was ruled by a powerful family known as the Plantagenets. The Plantagenets were a fascinating family that ruled England for about three hundred years and produced fourteen kings. Their triumphs and struggles shaped the country and would have a lasting impact that the Tudors had to deal with when they took the throne.

The Plantagenet kings were bold, dynamic, and powerful. They also fought viciously amongst themselves for control of the country. Some of the Plantagenet kings were legendary and greatly beloved by their citizens, while some of them were so brutal or ineffective that they caused widespread revolts. Understanding the effect that the Plantagenets had on England will help modern readers understand why the Tudors made certain decisions and what challenges they faced when they established a new dynasty.

The Plantagenets

The Plantagenet family was founded in Anjou, France. The name Plantagenet began as a nickname for Geoffrey, Count of Anjou, in the 12th century. The Plantagenets became viable contenders for the English throne during a violent time in English history known as the Anarchy.

The Anarchy was a vicious civil war that nearly tore England apart. In 1120, Henry I's only son died when his ship sank. King Henry I decided that he would make his daughter, Matilda, his heir, but this was a difficult process. She became known as Empress Matilda, but much of the nobility opposed her succession. When Henry I died in 1135, his nephew, Stephen Blois, claimed the crown. This would eventually lead to the Anarchy, which lasted from 1138 to 1153. Empress Matilda and Stephen fought bitterly while the country descended into chaos. At that time, the country was controlled by barons who fought each other and grabbed power while Matilda and Stephen were otherwise occupied. Many people died, and packs of mercenaries bullied farmers and villagers.

Before the war, Empress Matilda married Geoffrey Plantagenet, Count of Anjou, and the two had a son, Henry. King Stephen also had a son named Eustace. Both sides fought to gain the throne for their sons. While Stephen fought against rebellious barons, the Welsh, and the Scots, he also had to deal with Matilda's multiple invasions. In time, Stephen controlled the southeast of England, Matilda controlled the southwest, and wealthy barons fought each other for the rest of England.

In 1143, Geoffrey conquered Normandy for Matilda. The war continued, and by 1150, even the power-hungry barons were tired of war. By that time, Matilda's son, who became known as Henry FitzEmpress, had invaded England. Stephen's son, Eustace, had died, and Stephen didn't have an heir. The church stepped in and negotiated the Treaty of Wallingford, which allowed Stephen to keep his throne but made Henry his successor. Both parties agreed to the truce, but Stephen didn't live long enough to enjoy the peace that the truce created. He died in 1154, which made Henry the king of England.

Henry II

Henry was born in 1133, and although his mother's claim to the throne was dismissed, he was still raised to become the next king of England. He married Eleanor of Aquitaine, who had been married to King Louis VII of France. She was a beautiful woman who would help him rule his territories effectively, and they made a formidable couple. When his father died in 1151, he became the duke of Normandy and the count of Anjou. He proceeded to invade England to claim his birthright and defeated the barons who refused to support him or give up their power. Thanks to the Treaty of Wallingford, he became King Stephen's heir, and in 1154, he inherited England and other territories, including Wales and Scotland.

1. Henry II

Henry was a natural leader who inspired men to fight for him, but he could be merciless when it was necessary. As soon as he was king, he began improving England and led the country as it recovered from the brutal years of the Anarchy. For years, the country had been terrorized by war, and it needed serious reformation. Henry quickly put administrative systems in place and reformed the judicial system. He increased England's borders through warfare as well as through diplomacy. He arranged suitable marriages for his children, and he gained territory in Castile, Sicily, Germany, and Normandy. While Henry II was a great king who led his country through difficult times, he was also a controlling and often insensitive man. This led to serious personal problems that led to serious consequences for his reign.

The first personal fight involved one of his closest advisors. Thomas Becket was Henry's trusted friend, and he proved to be a capable leader. Henry sought to control the church in England but needed someone who would be on his side to accomplish that goal. Thomas had already proved his worth several times before, so Henry helped Thomas become the archbishop of Canterbury in May 1162. Unfortunately, Thomas and Henry disagreed on several matters, and this led to a fight between the two. Thomas chose to be exiled, which was a serious inconvenience for Henry. Their feud ended tragically on December 29th, 1170, when Thomas Becket was murdered in Canterbury Cathedral by four knights. Henry was blamed for the murder, and he faced backlash from the church and his subjects.

During his reign, he had eight children with Eleanor: William, Henry, Geoffrey, Richard, John, Matilda, Eleanor, and Joan. Unfortunately, Henry, William, and Geoffrey died while they were still quite young. Thomas Becket's murder was exacerbated when Henry's own sons rebelled against him. The rebellion was backed by Eleanor of Aquitaine, King Louis VII of France, and King William, the Lion of Scotland. Henry managed to suppress the rebellion in 1174 and pardoned his sons. However, Eleanor wasn't pardoned; she was kept in custody until her husband died. His troubles were far from over, as another rebellion broke out in 1181 between his sons Richard and John. Richard later allied himself with the king of France against Henry II in 1189. This rebellion broke

Henry, and he stepped aside so his son could take the throne. Henry II died in 1189 with the knowledge that his sons were united against him and his wife was still in custody.

While his personal life was a mess, Henry II was a good king who managed to reform an almost broken country. Today, he is seen as a capable ruler.

Richard the Lionheart

Richard was Henry II's and Eleanor of Aquitaine's third son, and he was born in September 1157. He was known for being an impressive knight and politician. Due to his military successes during the Third Crusade, he inspired several myths and became known as a romantic hero. His early life was marked by rebellion, as he and his brothers repeatedly rebelled against their father. He ruled Gascony and Poitou from a young age, and he was known for being a brutal leader. The Gascons tried to expel Richard from the duchy, but the rebellion failed when Richard's brother, Henry, died in 1183.

2. Richard I (Richard the Lionheart)

As Henry II's heir, Richard stood to inherit England, Normandy, and Anjou. For much of his reign, Henry II struggled to assign his sons' inheritances, and his decisions were often met with rebellion. When Richard became Henry's heir, Henry asked Richard to give Aquitaine to John. Richard refused and made an alliance with King Philip II of France. In 1189, they led another force against Henry. The rebellion was successful, and Richard was named Henry's heir.

Although Richard had fought to become the king of England, he showed no real interest in ruling his kingdom and instead set his sights on joining the Third Crusade. As soon as he became king, he began selling government positions, land, and other assets to raise an army. In 1190, he set sail for the Holy Land. While en route to the Crusade, he stopped in Sicily and helped to negotiate the Treaty of Messina, which made Tancred of Lecce the king of Sicily. However, this offended the Germans. Richard also married Berengaria of Navarre, but their relationship was a formal one. They had no children together.

While Richard experienced great victories in the Holy Land, he was unable to capture Jerusalem. He also fought with other European leaders, including Leopold V, Duke of Austria, and Philip II. After securing a truce with Saladin in the Holy Land in 1192, Richard decided to go home. Unfortunately, the offenses that he caused in the Holy Land had disastrous results when his ship was driven off course. He found himself in Vienna. Duke Leopold captured him and eventually handed him over to Henry VI, the Holy Roman emperor. Henry VI imposed a heavy ransom on Richard of 150,000 marks. England was prospering at the time, so Richard was able to pay most of the ransom and return to his kingdom.

He returned to England on April 17th, 1194, and was crowned again. This was likely due to the fact that his brother, John, had been slowly usurping the throne in his absence. However, Richard didn't remain in England for very long and left for Normandy the next month. He wouldn't return from Normandy, though; he died due to a battle wound in 1199. Richard died without an heir, and his younger brother, John, succeeded him.

The Magna Carta

For years before Richard I died, John had tried to usurp the throne. As Henry I's youngest son, John was likely used to being overlooked when it came to receiving a fair inheritance. When Richard died without any heirs, John was able to seize the throne, but he was in a precarious position. Unlike his older brother, he wasn't an accomplished warrior, and his people were unhappy because of the taxes that had been imposed on them during Richard's reign.

John also failed to provide his barons and clergy with a general charter of their rights when he ascended to the throne. Starting with William the Conqueror, the kings of England always gave their barons and clergy promises of goodwill and granted them certain rights. This ensured that the nobility and the church stayed on the king's side. Since John neglected this serious duty, the barons began revolting early on in his reign. He faced another disaster when he lost Normandy in 1204. John began taxing his people more harshly to make up for the loss. This outraged his people, and he went further by taxing the church relentlessly. His mistreatment of the church was so serious that he was excommunicated in 1209.

Facing widespread rebellion, John was forced to negotiate a charter with the nobility. The fact that the nobility was willing to meet with the king was incredible because most of them wanted to fight for their rights, but William Marshal, Earl of Pembroke, managed to gather the most important members of the nobility. In 1215, John signed the Articles of the Barons, which met most of the barons' demands and curbed some of his power. By agreeing to their demands, John effectively avoided another civil war. While this document helped avoid an immediate civil war, further discussions were needed to satisfy the barons. Later that year, John signed the Charter of Liberties, which became known as the Magna Carta.

The Magna Carta had to be reissued three more times in 1216, 1217, and 1225. It was refined, and sections were added over the years, but the main purpose of the charter was to establish feudal law. The Magna Carta was also a symbolic document because it gave people hope and power to fight against oppression. It had a lasting effect on English history, and some of its clauses were later used to govern English colonies.

England vs. France

When Henry II ascended the English throne, he brought a lot of French territory with him, including the Duchy of Normandy and the Aquitaine lands. This land was passed on to his successors, but it was also a source of contention between England and France. While Henry II's sons were able to hold onto that land for a while, much of it was eventually lost when Philip II of France and Richard I fought for control. Richard I was able to keep his inherited lands, but his successor wasn't able to hold onto the lands for very long. In 1202, John lost Normandy and its surroundings to Philip II.

John didn't give up that easily, though. In 1213, he went to war against France. In 1214, Pope Innocent III formed an anti-France alliance, which John quickly joined. The English forces and their allies met Philip II at the Battle of Bouvines, where England was defeated. From there, France conquered Flanders, and much of England's continental lands were lost. It was a devastating blow, one that John wouldn't recover from, and he stopped trying to regain the lands his predecessors had used to make England rich.

It did not, however, end the conflict between England and France, as the House of Plantagenet would not give up on their Angevin lands that easily. The two countries had a long and contentious history, and the Battle of Bouvines wouldn't be the last time that England and France met on the battlefield. The wars between the two countries had a disastrous impact on ordinary people, as they had to give up sons to become soldiers, were taxed mercilessly, and had to deal with armies marching through their lands and farms. The residents who lived in Angevin lands had to deal with upheaval since they were usually caught in the middle of the conflicts.

Edward I

While the Magna Carta was supposed to establish feudal law, John mostly ignored the charter. He was a widely unpopular king. When he died, his son, Henry, inherited a country that was on the brink of civil war. He was largely considered to be an ineffectual king, and his reign was riddled with problems. King John treated his barons terribly, which led to the Barons' Wars, which Henry was able to resolve, but he also suffered many losses on the battlefield. His military failures caused him to impose harsh taxes on his people, but they rebelled against him. He was taken prisoner by Simon de Montfort in 1264. In 1265, Henry III was rescued by his son, Edward. Once Henry III was freed, he took an interest in architecture and allowed his son to take over many of his duties.

As a young man, Edward I gained a reputation for being a harsh ruler and was known for having a violent temper. However, he was born to be a king and displayed many noble qualities. He was so tall that he gained the nickname "Longshanks," and he proved to be a capable warrior when he strengthened his father's rule and defeated Wales. Unlike King John, he upheld the Magna Carta and spent a lot of time securing his rule in England. He built several magnificent castles and joined the Crusades for some time. While he was a prince, he married Eleanor of Castile. The couple had four sons and eleven daughters together. When she died, he built twelve monuments in her honor.

3. Edward I

While he was a good English king, he was also an ambitious man and set his sights on Scotland. Unfortunately for him, the Scots proved difficult to subdue, and his actions caused friction between the two countries that would endure long after he had died. His attacks on Scotland earned him the nickname "Hammer of the Scots." He died on July 7th, 1307, while en route to Scotland and was succeeded by his son, Edward II.

Edward I left England in a relatively strong position, but his heir proved to be a spectacular failure. He seemed more interested in spending time with his friends than ruling his country. He essentially allowed his kingdom to fall into chaos. In 1314, Edward II was defeated by Robert the Bruce at the Battle of Bannockburn, effectively shattering Edward I's hope of conquering Scotland. In 1327, his wife, Isabella of France, forced him to abdicate. Edward II was imprisoned by his wife and her lover, Roger Mortimer. The king was later murdered, and historians suspect that Isabella and Roger were guilty of regicide.

King Arthur and the Impact of Chivalry

By the 12th century, the legend of King Arthur had a massive impact on England's overall culture. The literature of the period created the idea of a chivalrous knight who was a hero and only used his weapons to defend the helpless. The ideal knight was also a poet and a musician. The literature also included the concept of courtly love, which was an intricate social practice that was emphasized by chivalry. A hero could only win over his lady love if he was a man of exceptional courtesy, sportsmanship, generosity, and poetry.

The legend of Lancelot, one of King Arthur's knights, exemplified chivalry. Lancelot was known for being the greatest knight, with all other knights seeking to imitate him. He was a kind man who never lost control, except when it came to his true love, Queen Guinevere. Their relationship is also an example of how popular tragedies were during this period. Lancelot and Guinevere were doomed lovers, and this fact made their story incredibly popular.

Medieval knights were an important part of the social hierarchy. Knights were sworn to lords and were sworn to uphold the Knights Code of Chivalry. The code was supposed to ensure that knights would always protect the helpless, but many knights simply ignored the code. Knights would fight for their lords in battles and took part in tournaments. Tournaments were essentially war games that included jousts and group combat. Sometimes, the fighting became so fierce that men died. In time, tournaments became fairs that included entertainment such as dancing and feasting.

Medieval England was a dangerous place. While knights were supposed to protect the general population, they often took advantage of times of chaos and anarchy to bully the local countryside. While chivalry was a popular concept, many people died brutally and were subject to the violent tempers of the Plantagenet kings. In time, the Plantagenet dynasty would come to an end but not before the Hundred Years' War with France and the brutal Wars of the Roses. The Tudors were nearly extinguished during those chaotic years, but due to the actions of a few shrewd individuals, the Wars of the Roses would end with a Tudor on the throne.

Chapter 2: The Origins of the House of Tudor

The House of Tudor was a noble house with ties to the Welsh, French, and English royal families. It was uniquely situated to take hold of the English crown, but several things needed to happen before its claim could be considered legitimate. When the family was founded, no one could have imagined the heights that would be achieved by their descendants. The Tudor dynasty began in Wales in a village named Penmynydd. From the beginning, the family was involved in politics, but they were mostly involved in local matters and Welsh state of affairs. While the family eventually split into different branches, the most prominent branch descended from a Welsh courtier named Owen Tudor, who captured the heart of a queen.

To fully understand how the Tudors rose to power, it is important to understand how the mighty House of Plantagenet fell apart. While the Plantagenets had risen to dizzying heights under Henry II, their lineage weakened through the rule of weak and ineffectual kings. The Plantagenets were famous for their stubborn and violent tempers. The great kings either overcame their tempers or used their passion to motivate them. However, weaker kings indulged in petty vices and brought the kingdom to the brink of destruction. While matters looked bleak for the Plantagenets after the disastrous reign of Edward II, another great king was on the horizon. Edward III would usher in another age of prosperity for the Plantagenets, but his death would effectively rip the dynasty apart, paving the way for the Tudors to take the English throne.

Edward III

Edward III inherited a country that had slipped into chaos. After all, his mother had become his father's greatest enemy (and possible murderer). He didn't have the easiest upbringing or succession, but Edward III went on to accomplish great things. Edward was able to unify the barons and strengthen the country. However, his rule was also beset by problems, such as the Hundred Years' War with France, the Black Plague, and a corrupt government influenced by his thieving mistress, Alice Perrers.

4. King Edward III

Edward III was born in 1312 in Windsor Castle, but he spent most of his childhood in France with his mother since his parents had a strained relationship. While in France, Isabella took to wearing black, declaring that her marriage with her husband was dead. She took a lover named Roger Mortimer. Together, they plotted to take the throne from Edward II, who was extremely unpopular in England. In October 1326, Isabella and Roger invaded England, and Edward II was forced to abdicate early the next year. Edward III was crowned at fourteen years of age, but his mother and Roger Mortimer acted as his regents.

The couple planned on ruling England through the boy and began enriching themselves as soon as he was coronated. However, Edward III had different plans. In 1330, he had Roger Mortimer imprisoned in the Tower of London, where he was later executed for treason. Isabella was imprisoned in Norfolk. Edward III began ruling in earnest with his wife, Philippa of Hainault, and the pair had thirteen children. Their oldest son, Edward, became a famous knight who won many victories in France. Together, father and son gained incredible glory for their kingdom. England's future seemed bright, especially since the two established a new era of chivalry.

Edward III proved to be a good warrior and revived the military aspirations of previous English kings. He fought against David II of Scotland, but in 1336, he turned his attention to France. In the 1330s, Edward III boldly claimed the right to inherit the French throne. Since his mother belonged to the French royal family, he had the right to inherit the throne through her, but the French didn't recognize his claim since they preferred to recognize the patrilineal lineage. So, while Edward was Charles IV's closest living male relative, the French chose to recognize Philip VI as the new king of France. Edward III's claim to the throne led to violent wars between the French and English that lasted for over a century.

Unfortunately, that war led to the death of Edward III's heir, Edward the Black Prince. Edward III ruled for half a century, and his reign led to a golden era that enriched his country. Unfortunately, as he got older, he lost the keen senses that helped him become a great king. Toward the end of his reign, he took a mistress named Alice Perrers. While his health declined, the government began to slip into corruption, which caused Edward to become unpopular among his subjects. The English Parliament decided to clean up the government and identified the main culprits behind the spread of corruption. This decision would lead to serious consequences for Edward III's successors.

However, Edward III wouldn't feel those consequences, as he had a stroke in 1376 and died the following year. He was succeeded by Richard II, who had to fight against his uncle, John of Gaunt, Duke of Lancaster.

The Hundred Years' War

The Hundred Years' War was a brutal and costly war. During it, several English and French kings fought for dominance of the Angevin lands. The war started out relatively simple, pitting Edward III against Philip VI of France. Instead of declaring war outright, Edward III claimed his right to the French throne, which would have prevented the intervention of the church since he had the right to inherit through his mother, Isabella. Philip VI didn't take the claim lightly. In 1340, he sent a fleet of ships to attack England, but he lost most of his ships at Sluys in the Scheldt estuary.

When the two kings met on land, Edward III offered to solve the matter with a duel, which reflected the culture of military chivalry that Edward III upheld. Over the next few years, Edward III gained an advantage in the war. In 1345, English forces captured Gascony, and in 1347, Edward III gained the port of Calais. Philip VI tried to strike back by persuading the Scottish to invade the north of England, which would force Edward III to invade and make him fight on two fronts. The Scottish obliged, but their king, David II, was captured in battle. Later, in the midst of the devastation of the

Black Plague, Philip VI's successor, John II, fought against the English but was captured by the Black Prince in battle.

In 1359, Edward III marched to France with the intention of becoming the French king, but his troops were laid low by harsh weather conditions. So, he changed tactics and began negotiating a treaty. The Treaty of Brétigny recognized Edward III's claims to land in France, and Edward III withdrew his claim to the French throne. However, things were far from over. Edward III soon learned that he couldn't hold onto his French lands. His rule was beset by the Black Plague, and John II's successor, Charles V, proved to be a wily enemy who slowly claimed Edward III's lands in France.

Edward III started a war that he wouldn't be able to finish, which eventually drained the English treasury and cost hundreds of thousands of lives. When Edward III died, his successors would continue their father's fight, and it would leave a lasting mark on English history.

The Black Death

The war in France had to be halted when a more serious threat arrived on European shores. The bubonic plague was brought to Europe when ships from the Black Sea docked at Messina in Sicily. Most of the sailors aboard the ships were dead, and the port authorities had no idea what had just hit them. From there, the Black Plague spread like wildfire and killed up to 30 to 50 percent of Europe's population. England wasn't immune, and in 1348, the Black Death struck. Edward III's ambitions had to be put on hold as the plague ripped through his ranks and destroyed his workforce.

The effects were disastrous. Entire families, skilled laborers, and craftsmen all succumbed to the disease. The European economy took a massive dip, and kings had to stop fighting each other to try and save their people. Edward III wasn't immune to the effects of the plague, as his daughter, Joan, died from it. While dealing with personal tragedy, he had to find ways to revive the economy and guide his people through the deadliest pandemic in history. Unfortunately, the Black Death would have lasting consequences on Edward III's efforts to hold onto the lands granted to him in the Treaty of Brétigny. People died quickly due to the plague, and the greatly reduced population meant that it was harder to get soldiers and workers who could advance English interests in France.

It also meant that there were fewer Englishmen to occupy the lands in France and protect themselves from invading French forces. While Edward III and his son, Edward the Black Prince, won massive victories at the beginning of the Hundred Years' War, they were laid low by the sheer devastation of the Black Plague. Europe would never be the same after the Black Death. Millions of people died, and it left destruction in its wake. The impact of the war and the plague were so severe that Edward III was forced to declare bankruptcy in the 1340s. England was able to recover in time, but a new era in Plantagenet history was about to arrive shortly after the death of Edward the Black Prince and Edward III. The mighty House of Plantagenet found itself divided into the House of Lancaster and the House of York, which would eventually spell disaster for the Plantagenet line.

House of Lancaster

The House of Lancaster was founded when Henry III (r. 1216-1272) made his youngest son, Edmund, the earl of Lancaster. Unfortunately, both of Edmund's sons died, which meant that the lands passed to his granddaughters, Maud and Blanche. Maud died soon after her father, and Blanche married John of Gaunt, who was Edward III's son. John had been involved in the corruption scandal that erupted toward the end of Edward III's reign, but he still held a lot of power at court when his nephew became king.

5. House of Lancaster insignia

When Edward III died, his grandson, Richard II, took the throne. He was only ten years old at the time, and he inherited a crown that was deeply in debt. The government's response was to impose a heavy tax on the people, which led to the Peasants' Revolt a few years after Richard's coronation. Despite his young age, he successfully ended the revolt, but this was likely due to the efforts of his advisors. As Richard's reign continued, he slowly alienated himself from his high-ranking nobles. Meanwhile, the House of Lancaster under John Gaunt, Edward III's son, began gaining power. Richard II eventually became a harsh tyrant who was determined to enhance his own prestige as king.

In 1399, John of Gaunt died, and his son, Henry, deposed Richard II and became King Henry IV. The king merged his Lancastrian inheritance with the throne, and for the next sixty years, England was ruled by the Lancastrians. Henry IV was succeeded by his son, Henry V, who experienced great success in the Hundred Years' War. In 1415, he won the historic Battle of Agincourt, which made him one of the most popular kings in English history. In 1420, he signed the Treaty of Troyes, which named Henry as

Charles VI's heir. He married Catherine of Valois, who later went on to marry Owen Tudor.

Henry V's success in the Hundred Years' War locked him and his descendants into further conflicts, especially against the Dauphin Charles, who was Charles VI's original heir. The war in France heated up, and Henry V was forced to join the fighting again in 1422, which was the year he died. Unfortunately for England, Henry V died young. His son, Henry VI, was little more than a baby. Henry VI wasn't as successful as his father, and the French soon gained strong leaders, such as Joan of Arc, which turned the tide against England.

Unlike his father, Henry VI wasn't interested in continuing the war against France, and in 1445, he married Margaret of Anjou. In time, Henry VI became unfit to rule, as he was seized by a mysterious illness that left him unresponsive for over a year. It was during this time that the House of York seized the opportunity to take the throne.

The House of York

The House of York was founded by Edward III's son, Edmund Langley. The first two dukes of York didn't do much but rule their duchy. When Edmund's son, Edward, died without an heir, his assets and title were passed to his nephew, Richard. The new duke of York was related to Edward III's son, Lionel, which gave him a prestigious lineage. Richard set his sights on further glory when Henry VI slipped into madness. During that time, the throne was controlled by Margaret of Anjou.

6. House of York insignia

Margaret's rule was largely unpopular, and Richard was a direct descendant of Edward III, which made his claim legitimate. Both the House of Lancaster and the House of York could claim rights to the throne since they could trace their lineage back to Edward III. The House of York had ties to Lionel, Duke of Clarence, who was John of Gaunt's older brother. Meanwhile, the House of Lancaster was directly descended from John of Gaunt. The crown was in a precarious position since the Lancaster king, Henry VI, was weakened by his mysterious illness, and Margaret of Anjou was proving to be an ineffectual regent.

For years, Richard, the 3rd Duke of York, tried to work with Henry VI's government, but he eventually decided to claim the throne. Parliament arranged a compromise in which Henry would remain king, but Richard would inherit the throne when Henry died. Both parties were appeased, and Henry VI accepted the act. However, Margaret of Anjou didn't accept the treaty since it would disinherit her own son. These factors would eventually lead to the Wars of the Roses, which would destabilize the country and lead to a new dynasty.

While the Lancastrians and Yorkists were heading to war, the Lancastrians found themselves at a disadvantage due to a distinct lack of male heirs. They found a solution to this problem through the marriage of Margaret Beaufort and Edmund Tudor. Margaret Beaufort was a descendant of John of Gaunt, while Edmund Tudor was Henry VI's half-brother and a descendant of the House of Valois, the French royal house.

Owen Tudor

Owen Tudor was a descendant of the Welsh Tudor family, which was heavily involved in the Welsh government. The family first rose to prominence in Wales under Ednyfed Fychan, who worked under Llywelyn the Great. His loyal service to the monarch earned him vast lands in northern Wales, which included Penmynydd. This became the family's seat of power. The Tudors allied themselves with Edward I and remained loyal supporters of the English royal house. However, in time, the family joined Owain Glyndwr, who rebelled against the English in the early 1400s. They were soundly defeated, and the Tudors lost much of their land. Many members of the family were executed for treason. Thankfully, Owen Tudor was able to rise above this failure and went on to work for Henry V.

7. House of Tudor genealogy chart

His background is famously obscure, but historians know that he was born around 1400, and he was the son of Maredudd Tudor. In time, Owen became the keeper of the queen of England's wardrobe. When Henry V died, his wife, Catherine of Valois, was still a beautiful young woman who faced early retirement. Catherine and Owen fell in love and married without permission. They were able to keep their marriage secret for a few years, during which time they had five children: three sons and two daughters.

Unfortunately, when their secret was discovered, Catherine was exiled to a nunnery, and Owen was imprisoned in Newgate Prison. However, he managed to escape and returned to Wales. Catherine died in the nunnery around 1437, while Owen returned to Wales in 1438. When Henry VI was threatened by Yorkist forces in 1461, Owen took an army to support the king. Owen was captured by the Yorkists and was executed in Hereford. Although he was beheaded as a prisoner of war, the Tudor dynasty had already begun. Owen and Catherine's sons, Edmund and Jasper, would help raise the House of Tudor to glory, and their descendants would usher in another golden age in England's history.

Jasper and Edmund Tudor

Catherine of Valois was only twenty years old when her husband died, and ambitious nobles immediately set their sights on the dowager queen. In response, English Parliament forbade her from marrying without a special license and express permission from the king. However, Catherine and Owen Tudor fell in love and ignored this law. They had several children, but the two most influential were Edmund and Jasper. After their mother died, they were placed in the care of Katherine de la Pole, and they were eventually called to court by their half-brother, Henry VI.

Henry VI declared Edmund and Jasper legitimate and made Edmund the earl of Richmond, while Jasper became the earl of Pembroke. In 1453, they were officially recognized as the king's brothers. They both received large portions of land, and in 1454, they were made Lady Margaret Beaufort's wards. She was the sole heiress of her father's immense fortune. Edmund married her in 1455 when he was twenty-nine years old, and she was only twelve. At that time, the Yorkists were already gaining power, and the War of the Roses was looming.

8. Margaret Beaufort

During that time period, it wasn't unusual for girls to be married off at a young age, but to protect her, their husbands were ordered to wait until the girl was at least fourteen years old before they began trying for an heir. Edmund ignored this rule, and Margaret became pregnant soon after their marriage.

Once the Wars of the Roses began, Edmund and Jasper fought for King Henry VI, but Edmund was captured in 1456 by Yorkists and taken to Carmarthen Castle in Wales. He died from the plague later that year. Jasper took Margaret to Pembroke Castle, where she gave birth to a son. She was still only twelve years old, and the process was extremely traumatic. Margaret was never able to have children again, despite the fact that she got married two more times after. Despite her difficult early years, Margaret became a formidable figure in the War of the Roses and was instrumental in helping her son gain the English throne.

The War of the Roses had begun, and while the Yorkists had the advantage at first, the future king of England, Henry VII, had just been born. Through his mother and father, Henry Tudor had connections to the royal houses of France, Wales, and England, and he already had two formidable supporters in the form of Margaret Beaufort and Jasper Tudor.

Chapter 3: The Tudors' Rise to Power

The Wars of the Roses began in 1455, and by that time, the days of Plantagenet glory were long gone. The mighty ruling house had been divided into the Houses of York and Lancaster, which were about to rip into each other and cause one of the bloodiest civil wars in history. By the end of the civil war, about half of England's noble houses were gone. The House of Plantagenet came to a brutal end when the last Plantagenet heir, Edward, 17th Earl of Warwick, was executed in the Tower of London.

9. Battle of Towton, Wars of the Roses

During the decades-long war, several influential individuals rose to power and influenced the course of history. People like the Kingmaker, Richard Neville, were able to become major players. While some of the central figures of the war were at the forefront of the action, some players, like Margaret Beaufort, kept to the shadows and manipulated events to their advantage. Many noble families were decimated, but others gained incredible fortunes, such as the infamous Woodvilles. It was a time of intense upheaval, brutal battles, and terrible losses, but it led to the foundation of the Tudor dynasty.

The Beginning of the Wars of the Roses

The Wars of the Roses were named after the white rose that represented the House of York and the red rose that represented the House of Lancaster. Before the catastrophic civil wars, the House of Lancaster ruled England through Henry VI. He was the son of the great king, Henry V, and due to his father's untimely death, he became the king of England while he was still an infant. There were high hopes for his rule, but unlike his father, Henry VI wasn't a natural leader and didn't seem too interested in his kingly duties. In time, his nobles decided to take matters into their own hands.

As Henry VI's rule progressed, he lost many hard-won lands in France, which enraged his nobles, many of whom had fought alongside Henry V to gain them. In 1450, his people rebelled against him as a result of heavy taxes. The rebellion was led by Jack Cade, who demanded that the king allow Richard of York to return to England. Richard of York was also a descendant of Richard III and could make a claim to the throne.

Henry VI refused, and he eventually defeated the rebellion. For much of his reign, Henry VI and his wife, Margaret of Anjou, were influenced by the duke of Somerset, Edmund Beaufort. This blatant favoritism caused friction within the court. When Richard of York returned to England in 1452, he urged Henry VI to fire

Edmund Beaufort. Unfortunately for Richard, Margaret gave birth to Edward of Lancaster in 1453, which put Richard one step further away from the throne. By then, tensions were running high in England, and the Yorkists and Lancastrians were already beginning to fight with each other.

10. Richard of York

In 1454, disaster struck the House of Lancaster when Henry VI slipped into a state of catatonic madness. Richard was appointed as the Lord Protector of England. Richard wasted little time and quickly began putting his own allies into positions of power within the government. During this time, Margaret of Anjou and Richard of York became clear enemies.

Henry VI managed to recover by 1455, but the damage was done. The stage was set for the Wars of the Roses. A few months after Henry VI recovered, he was forced to meet Richard of York and Richard Neville, Earl of Warwick, in battle at St. Albans. The Lancastrians were soundly defeated. Somerset was killed, and Henry was taken prisoner. Richard became the Lord Protector of England again while Margaret and her son fled into exile.

It was the first battle in a long civil war, but important alliances had already been created. Richard of York and Richard Neville were a force to be reckoned with, and Richard Neville's efforts on behalf of the House of York earned him the nickname "Kingmaker."

The Kingmaker

Richard Neville was born in 1428 and became the earl of Warwick in 1449. In 1453, he made an alliance with Richard of York and became one of his most important allies. Although the Yorkists scored a crucial victory at the Battle of St. Albans, their problems were far from over. Henry VI was a weak king who wasn't suited to rule or strengthen his throne through war, but his wife was ambitious and wanted to secure the throne for her son. When her most trusted ally, Edmund Beaufort, was killed, she took matters into her own hands. For the next few years, she raised armies to fight against the House of York.

11. Richard Neville, Earl of Warwick

In 1459, the House of Lancaster defeated the House of York, and Richard of York was forced to return to Ireland. However, things were far from over. Richard returned in 1460, and the

Yorkists were able to capture Henry. In an effort to avoid more fighting, Parliament passed the Act of Accord, which named Richard Henry VI's successor. Henry VI would be allowed to keep the crown until he died, but then the throne would pass to the House of York. This seemed like a fair compromise to most of the involved parties, but Margaret of Anjou didn't accept the Act of Accord.

This led to one of the most brutal battles in the entire civil war. Margaret led an army against the House of York, and the two armies met at Wakefield Green. For years, Margaret had been forced to run for her life and fight for her son's inheritance. The Battle of Wakefield was supposed to cement the York inheritance, but Richard was defeated by Margaret's army. Margaret showed no mercy and had Richard beheaded. However, she wasn't satisfied with Richard's execution. She took it one step further by having his head (wearing a paper crown) mounted on Micklegate Bar. This brutality shocked the country and mobilized her enemies against her.

Richard of York's sons joined the fight, and his oldest son, Edward, became a new contender for the throne. Backed by Richard Neville, Earl of Warwick, Edward fought against Margaret's forces a few more times but was defeated at the Battle of Mortimer's Cross and the Second Battle of St. Albans. In 1461, both sides met at Towton and engaged in one of the bloodiest battles in English history. Once the fighting was done, Margaret was on the run again. Edward IV was crowned the king of England.

Warwick had been Edward's strongest supporter, and his tireless efforts helped earn Edward his crown. He was given great honor and wealth in Edward's new government, and Warwick began negotiating with European powers to get Edward a bride with the hopes of building a powerful alliance. However, Edward had other ideas, and his choice of a wife would cause catastrophic consequences. In time, Warwick set his sights on putting the

Lancastrians back in power, and he helped Henry VI return to the throne in 1470. Warwick was an ambitious and manipulative individual who put two men on the throne to further his own causes.

Edward IV

Edward IV wasn't born to be king, but he was crowned in 1461 following the Battle of Towton. The Wars of the Roses had been raging for about six years at that point, and he had lost his father to the fighting. For the first few years of his reign, he remained in London while Warwick fought against the Lancastrians. It was clear that Warwick was the most powerful man in the realm. Things were about to change, though, as Edward was growing tired of submitting to Warwick and began looking for ways to distance himself from his advisor.

Warwick was determined to keep his power and began negotiations with the French to find Edward a French princess who would become his bride. Instead, Edward married Elizabeth Woodville in 1464. Elizabeth was extremely beautiful, but she was the widow of a defeated Lancastrian noble and already had two sons. Her own mother, Jacquetta, had served Margaret of Anjou at court. This marriage caused a massive rift between Edward and Warwick. Edward quickly began giving Woodvilles positions in power, which helped build his own power. Warwick quickly lost power and favor, which incensed him. In 1469, he sought to regain his power by capturing Edward IV in battle. He kept the king prisoner, but Edward IV escaped. Warwick was forced to flee to France, where he set up an alliance with Margaret of Anjou.

Warwick and his allies fought against Edward in 1471, and Edward had to retreat. In 1471, the two met in battle again, and Warwick was killed. Margaret of Anjou arrived in England just as Warwick was defeated. The two armies met at Tewkesbury, and Margaret was confident that her side would win. Finally, her son, Edward, Prince of Wales, would be crowned king. Edward IV defeated the Lancastrians, and Margaret's son was killed, much to her horror. When Edward returned to London, he "learned" that Henry VI had died in the Tower of London soon before his arrival. (The Yorkists claimed that the old king died of sadness, but it is more likely that he was murdered on Edward's orders.)

For the rest of his reign, Edward IV concentrated on enriching his kingdom and improving law enforcement. The country had been ravaged by wars, and his efforts helped stabilize the country again. His reign was extremely successful, and he had seven children with Elizabeth Woodville. They had two sons, Edward and Richard, as well as five daughters. The oldest daughter, Elizabeth of York, would become an important component in the unification of the Houses of York and Lancaster. During Edward IV's reign, the kingdom enjoyed peace and prosperity, but unfortunately, the Wars of the Roses were far from over.

The Boys in the Tower

Richard of York had three sons: Edward, George, and Richard. When Edward became king, he made George the duke of Clarence, and Richard became the duke of Gloucester. During the early years of Edward's reign, he enjoyed the support of his brothers. However, during his ongoing struggle against Warwick, George changed sides and joined Warwick. Although George betrayed Edward, he was eventually pardoned. Unfortunately, George didn't learn his lesson and betrayed Edward again. In 1478, Edward was forced to execute his brother.

Richard remained loyal to his brother and king, and before Edward died in 1483, he appointed Richard as the Lord Protector of England. As soon as Edward died, his son, Edward V, was appointed king immediately. Edward V was only twelve years old, and Richard was supposed to rule as protector until Edward was old enough to rule. However, Edward's mother, Elizabeth Woodville, had him crowned immediately, likely to inhibit Richard's power.

12. The princes in the Tower

This would have allowed the Woodvilles to rule England through Edward V. Richard was far too ambitious to allow that to happen. In 1483, he met the Earl of Rivers at Stony Stratford and placed the earl in prison before taking Edward with him. Once in London, he was declared the Lord Protector and placed Edward in the Tower of London. Elizabeth and her children sought shelter in Westminster Abbey with her remaining children, but on June 16th, Richard had Edward's younger brother also taken to the Tower. It was becoming increasingly apparent that Richard wasn't going to give up his power.

On June 26th, he made a claim to the throne by declaring that Edward IV's sons were illegitimate. Richard became Richard III, and he was crowned the king of England in early July. However, his rule was far from secure since Edward IV's sons were still alive in the Tower of London. Most people were shocked by Richard's actions. The situation worsened when both boys simply disappeared. Richard was now undisputedly the king of England. No one knows what happened to his nephews. Edward V was never heard from again, but several pretenders claimed to be his younger brother, Richard. Richard III was now the most powerful man in England, but his nephews' disappearance made him wildly unpopular.

Richard III

Richard III was Edward IV's youngest brother. While he was born into wealth and was well connected, he didn't stand to inherit much, and his future didn't look very bright. However, when the Wars of the Roses began, he and his brothers were supposed to become Henry VI's heirs. When their father died and Edward became king, Richard became a prince and was made the duke of Gloucester. Richard and George were placed in Warwick's care until they were old enough to take over their estates.

When he entered adulthood, the Wars of the Roses had resumed when Warwick fought against Edward IV. While George and Warwick turned against Edward, Richard remained loyal to his brother. When Edward IV defeated George and Warwick, he rewarded Richard's loyalty by appointing him as the king's representative in Wales. Throughout Edward's reign, Richard remained loyal and fought on Edward's side during several key battles against the Lancastrians. As a result, Edward lavished lands on his brother, mostly giving him lands in the north of England, which strengthened Richard's power considerably. Later, Richard married Warwick's youngest daughter, Anne Neville, and received most of Warwick's lands.

Richard was very popular in the north, but his growing power worried several nobles, including the queen, Elizabeth Woodville. When Edward IV died, there were fears that Richard would use his position as Lord Protector to essentially rule the country, so the queen had her son, Edward V, declared the king of England. Unfortunately, Richard usurped the throne, and his nephews mysteriously vanished. Since Richard had the most to gain from their disappearance, people suspected that he had his nephews murdered.

During his reign, Richard tried to be a good king and abolished some of Edward IV's unpopular edicts, such as forced gifts from nobles. However, he faced unrest in the south of England, the threat of invasion from France, and economic hardship. He found that ruling England was much harder than ruling his own lands in the north. Disaster struck in 1483 when many Yorkists deserted him, and the south of England rebelled against him. He managed to stop the rebellion, but many nobles, including the Woodvilles, went to Brittany, where they supported Henry Tudor's claim to the throne. In 1484, his son (and only child) died, leaving him without an heir. The next year, his wife also died.

In the midst of these tragedies, Richard found a seemingly perfect solution. He planned to marry his niece, Elizabeth of York, Edward IV's oldest daughter. Elizabeth was young and beautiful, which would provide Richard with a chance to have another heir and would strengthen his claim to the throne. While his plan was perfect on paper, it was very unpopular, and his supporters quickly dwindled. While his supporters could stomach the disappearance of Richard's nephews, they drew the line at allowing the king to marry his niece. Richard never ended up marrying Elizabeth.

While Richard III desperately looked for ways to keep ruling England, Henry Tudor was gathering support for his own claim to the throne. The Yorkists had successfully kept their power for most of the Wars of the Roses, but they had turned on each other and fought amongst themselves until they made their cause unpopular. The Lancastrians had been forced to bide their time, and as Richard III struggled to keep his throne, they saw their chance.

Margaret Beaufort

While the Wars of the Roses raged on, Margaret Beaufort went from a child to an influential player in some of the most dramatic events during the bloody civil war. When she was just twelve or thirteen years old, she gave birth to Henry Tudor. From then on, she was committed to securing her son's inheritance. Unlike Margaret of Anjou, Margaret Beaufort used subtle tactics to further her cause.

When her husband, Edmund Tudor, died, she was betrothed to Sir Henry Stafford, who was the duke of Buckingham. Margaret was forced to leave her son with Jasper Tudor for his own safety since he was a Lancastrian heir with ties to the throne during a time when the Yorkists were quickly gaining power. As the only child of John Beaufort, Margaret was an extremely wealthy heiress, but when Edward IV became king, he took her lands and gave them to his brother, George. She campaigned to have her lands returned to her, but she wasn't successful. When Henry VI was defeated at the Battle of Barnet, Margaret helped Jasper and Henry Tudor flee from England when Henry was only thirteen years old.

In 1472, Margaret married Lord Thomas Stanley after Lord Stafford died a year earlier at the Battle of Barnet. She was allowed to join Edward IV's court, where she sought the king's permission to allow her son to return to England. She became close to Elizabeth Woodville during this time. When Edward IV died and Richard III became king, she served in Queen Anne's court but secretly worked with Elizabeth Woodville to make her son, Henry, king.

Elizabeth Woodville had lost both of her sons but didn't allow her loss to force her into a quiet retirement. In 1483, she played a prominent role in Buckingham's rebellion, and Henry was set to invade England to help Buckingham. Unfortunately, the plan failed, and Margaret was almost executed. Richard III ordered her husband, Lord Stanley, to make sure that Margaret was isolated at one of his estates and cut off communication between her and her son. Margaret outwitted the king and managed to continue corresponding with her son. Lord Stanley was secretly on Margaret's side, and together, they arranged a new rebellion, which led to the Battle of Bosworth.

Margaret Beaufort managed to survive England's bloodiest civil war and founded a dynasty during times of incredible political upheaval. Not only did she survive when most of England's nobility went extinct, but she also managed to secure the English throne for her son.

The Unification of the York and Lancaster Dynasties

On August 22nd, 1485, Henry Tudor met Richard III at Bosworth. It would be the last battle of the Wars of the Roses, and everyone involved seemed to sense that things were coming to a head. Henry was supported by France and many English nobles, who had deserted Richard III. For thirty long years, England had been subjected to a series of battles that uprooted their way of life. The throne changed hands often, kings had been imprisoned, and heirs had been declared illegitimate as old scandals were dug up and exposed for political reasons. Finally, the Wars of the Roses were about to end. Henry Tudor won the battle, and Richard III was brutally killed. The battle inspired legendary stories, and apparently, the crown was taken from Richard's head and placed on Henry's.

Henry became Henry VII, but his troubles were far from over. The country was deeply divided after the civil war. In an effort to reunite the country, he married Edward IV's daughter, Elizabeth of York. The House of Tudor had taken the throne of England, but

Henry VII would have to face financial difficulties, rebellions, and personal tragedy during his reign. He faced an uphill battle from the start, but with some powerful allies, he was able to secure the Tudor dynasty and leave the throne in a stable position for his heirs.

Part Two: Monarchs and Royalty (1485–1603)

Chapter 4: Henry VII (r. 1485–1509)

When Henry VII was born, his future looked bleak. His mother was barely a teenager, and his father was dead. Due to the Wars of the Roses, his inheritance had been seized and distributed to other nobles. Things didn't look good for the Lancastrians; their king was mad, and their queen was brutal and ambitious. It was a miracle that Henry and his family survived at all, as power changed hands often. For most of the civil war, it looked as though they were on the losing side. However, his mother's shrewd politics and a series of vital alliances meant that the Tudors rose steadily in the background of the Wars of the Roses.

13. Henry VII

Finally, Henry Tudor returned from exile and won the crown of England. He faced many challenges to get the throne, and he would face even more hardships to keep the crown in his possession, especially since new kings had appeared seemingly overnight during the civil war. Thankfully, he had powerful allies and learned to be a good king. Thanks to his efforts, the Houses of York and Lancaster were reunited, and he led his country through the aftermath of the bloody civil war. Margaret Beaufort and others helped him get the throne, but it was up to him to prove himself worthy of their efforts.

Early Life

Henry Tudor was the son of Edmund Tudor and Margaret Beaufort. Through his parents, he had a rich and varied lineage. On his father's side, he was the grandson of a Welsh nobleman and a French princess and former queen of England. On his mother's side, he was the great-great-grandson of John of Gaunt, the son of

Edward III. When he was born, he was a distant Lancastrian heir behind Henry VI, Henry VI's son, and older male Beauforts. At first, it didn't appear as though he had a particularly bright future, but then the Wars of the Roses began in earnest. In one fell swoop, the Lancastrian line was jeopardized when Henry VI, his son, and the Beaufort line fell in battle. Suddenly, Henry Tudor's distant claim to the throne was the best that the Lancastrians could hope for.

While the deaths of the other Lancastrian heirs meant that Henry could hope for a chance to become the king of England, it also meant that he would be in grave danger during the Wars of the Roses. Soon after he was born, his mother, Margaret, married Sir Henry Stafford. Henry was left in the care of his uncle, Jasper Tudor, Earl of Pembroke. Jasper Tudor was a loyal Lancastrian who was devoted to his nephew's cause. Unfortunately for the Lancastrians, they were soundly defeated at the Battle of Tewkesbury in 1471, and the Yorkist line was firmly established when Edward IV took the throne. Henry and Jasper Tudor were forced to flee to Brittany, where it seemed that Henry would die in obscurity. However, the Wars of the Roses were far from over.

When Edward IV died, Richard III began plans to usurp the throne. The House of York was divided, and Henry's fortunes changed again. In an effort to build a strong alliance against Richard III, Henry was betrothed to Edward IV's oldest daughter, Elizabeth of York. This was an ingenious plan since it would reunite the Houses of York and Lancaster after nearly thirty years of civil war. Richard III had great plans for his reign, and he made plans to invade France, which motivated the French to support Henry's claim to the English throne. Henry Tudor had fled into exile when he was a young teenager, but in 1485, at the age of twenty-eight, he arrived on English soil with an army.

The Battle of Bosworth

When Richard III claimed the throne and his nephews went missing in the Tower of London, the Yorkist party was split in two. Many of the nobles were alarmed by Richard III's usurpation and were hesitant to support his rule. Meanwhile, Henry Tudor had grown into a strong young man with a good reputation. When his betrothal to Elizabeth of York was finalized, it seemed to many that he would be the better king. Richard III's people began to rebel against him, and Henry Tudor could finally fight back against the Yorkists.

In 1483, the duke of Buckingham, Henry Stafford, led a rebellion against Richard III and asked for Henry Tudor's support. The rebellion was crushed before Henry Tudor could aid the duke's efforts, but it wouldn't be Henry's last chance. In the meantime, the Lancastrians formed an alliance with Yorkists who had abandoned Richard III's court. Richard III dealt with a great loss in 1484 when his heir died, but that only helped the Lancastrian cause and strengthened Henry's claim. In 1485, Henry landed in Wales with a small army and marched into England. As he marched, more people joined his army, but he was still outnumbered when he met Richard's forces in Leicestershire at Bosworth Field.

Unfortunately for Richard, many nobles were tired of war. One of his most important allies, Henry Percy, Earl of Northumberland, refused to join the battle until he knew who was going to win. During the battle, a few more of Richard's allies left him to join Henry's side. When Richard realized that Henry Percy wasn't going to help him, he allegedly broke off from the main army with his knights and decided to kill Henry Tudor himself. Lord Stanley, Margaret Beaufort's husband and Henry's stepfather, had been waiting to see how the battle would pan out. When he saw that Richard had broken away from his main forces, he decided to intervene on Henry's behalf. Richard was surrounded by enemies and quickly killed.

According to legends about the battle, Richard III had worn a crown into battle, which was knocked off his head when he was killed. That same crown was then used to crown Henry VII on the battlefield. After spending his life fighting the Yorkists and years in exile, Henry established the Tudor dynasty. He was now the king of England.

Family Life

Henry's ascent to the throne had been difficult, but he faced even more serious challenges trying to secure his crown. The country had been ripped apart by civil war, and his most pressing task was uniting the Houses of York and Lancaster. This was achieved by marrying Elizabeth of York in 1486. Many powerful Yorkists were angry about the loss at the Battle of Bosworth and would later go on to launch rebellions against Henry VII, but by marrying Elizabeth of York, he strengthened his claim to the throne and won more allies.

14. Elizabeth of York

After their marriage, Henry VII used the Tudor rose as an emblem of unification. The Tudor rose was a mixture of the white and red roses that represented the Houses of York and Lancaster. When Richard III took the throne, he enacted the Titulus Regius, an act that declared the marriage of Edward IV and Elizabeth Woodville invalid. This made their children illegitimate and made Richard III the legal heir. As soon as he was able, Henry reversed that act, making Elizabeth of York and her siblings legitimate again. This move strengthened Henry's hold on the throne since he had married one of Edward IV's heirs.

15. Tudor rose

Elizabeth of York also helped her husband at court. Since Henry VII had spent most of his life in exile, he was largely unfamiliar with the English nobles. Elizabeth, on the other hand, had grown up among them as a princess. She was used to courtly life, and her father had been a good king, which probably helped her to be a good queen. The couple had seven children together, but only four survived to adulthood. They had two sons, Arthur and Henry, and two daughters, Margaret and Mary. Margaret went on to become the queen of Scotland, and Mary became the queen of France.

Thanks to Henry VII's marriage to Elizabeth of York, his family was secure, and his children could claim a noble heritage and wouldn't have to spend their childhoods in exile. However, his throne was far from secure, and more effort was required to bring peace to his war-torn country.

Policies and Economy

The Wars of the Roses had been expensive, and the royal treasury was often used to fund the wars of whichever king was in power at the time. When Henry came to the throne, he found that he was in a court that was foreign to him after a life of exile. He was aware that the nobles in England were used to changing regimes and that many Yorkists were looking for an opportunity to advance their cause. As a result, he felt that there weren't many people he could trust. He built up a close-knit council of allies who had proven that they were trustworthy. He used lawyers and clerics in specialized councils, which he personally oversaw. This allowed him to keep a tight hold on his kingdom's affairs.

Henry also saw the need to impress his reign on his people through extravagant tournaments. He began renovating major castles, such as Windsor Castle, Richmond Castle, Greenwich Palace, the Tower of London, and Westminster Abbey. These were expensive endeavors, and Henry didn't want to rely on money from Parliament and allies. He also needed a way to keep the nobles in line and decided to solve both problems through a series of financial policies that would both enrich the monarchy and prevent the nobles from becoming too powerful. Henry and his council set up a series of taxes, fines, and rents, which proved to be very useful. Misdemeanors were punished through fines, and large taxes were placed on nobles. He also encouraged exports and helped increase the health of the English economy.

Henry paid close attention to his relationships with other European powers and signed trade treaties with Spain, Portugal, Florence, Denmark, and the Netherlands. In 1489, he sent an army to help his allies in Brittany when France threatened to invade, but he received money from Charles VIII of France to stay out of his affairs. As Henry's reign progressed, he proved that he was a capable king and did wonders for the English economy. He was adept at making money, which helped to keep the throne and country stable. Instead of punishing nobles with violence and battles, he imposed massive fines on them, which was lucrative and effective.

While Henry's reign was mostly focused on peace, he still faced times of trouble. Several Yorkists hoped to return a York heir to the throne, and while it was a good move to legitimize Edward IV's children, it also meant that Edward IV's sons were the true heirs. And not everyone believed that the princes in the Tower were actually dead.

Edward of Warwick and Perkin Warbeck

Henry VII has been credited with bringing an end to the Wars of the Roses, but the aftermath of the civil wars haunted him for much of his reign. On top of that, he had been forced to spend most of his childhood in exile, and during that time, his family wasn't in power. This meant they couldn't spend that time gathering connections for his rule. When Henry finally ascended to the throne, he found himself in charge of a court that was basically foreign, and even though the Yorkists had been defeated, they had not given up. The problem was that there were still a few legitimate Yorkist heirs with good claims to the throne, and many were happy to believe that one of the York princes had survived their ordeal in the Tower of London. These factors led to a few serious rebellions during Henry VII's reign, some of which were led by pretenders who imitated the legitimate Yorkist heirs.

The first Yorkist heir with a legitimate claim to the throne was Edward of Warwick, Edward IV's nephew through his brother George, Duke of Clarence. As a boy, Edward, Earl of Warwick, was locked up in the Tower of London soon after Henry VII ascended to the throne. However, enterprising Yorkists spread a rumor that the child had escaped and built an uprising around him. Edward was still safely in the Tower while the rebellion gained popularity. It turned out that the rebellion was led by a boy, Lambert Simnel, who looked like Edward. The Yorkist force was defeated at the Battle of East Stoke in 1487. Henry VII pardoned Simnel and gave him a job in the royal kitchens.

Unfortunately, the next rebellion wasn't defeated so easily. A man pretending to be Richard, Duke of York, the son of Edward IV, appeared in Europe. He won the support of European kings who were eager to stir up rebellion in England. Many nobles defected to the man's cause, and Henry VII faced the threat of invasion. In 1497, the two opposing armies met in Cornwall, where the rebellion was defeated. The "duke" turned out to be a lowborn man named Perkin Warbeck. He was executed two years later.

Throughout Henry's reign, he faced minor and major rebellions, but he managed to defeat the rebels and keep a firm hold on his throne. He managed to end the Wars of the Roses at the beginning of his reign, but he lived under the shadow of the civil war for the rest of his life.

My Lady, the King's Mother

During the Wars of the Roses, Margaret Beaufort fought for her son's cause. When people forgot about his claim to the throne and discounted his significance, she quietly plotted and furthered his cause. She became a masterful politician out of necessity and helped her son become the most powerful man in the kingdom. He never forgot her help, and when he became king, he made her one of his advisors. Margaret received extraordinary precedence at Henry's court, and reports indicate that he relied heavily on her advice. When Henry married Elizabeth of York, Margaret's influence wasn't diminished. In fact, she was allowed to wear the same quality clothes as the queen. She also adopted the new title, "My Lady, the King's Mother."

Margaret didn't waste her influence on ordering new clothes and making her daughter-in-law's life difficult. She also enacted new legal acts. During the civil war, the victorious kings were allowed to take land from defeated nobles. Margaret had been a victim of this practice, so when her son was king, she made it illegal for the nobles and royals to steal land from each other. She also made it possible for her to take control of her own lands even though she was still married.

As Margaret grew older, she also invented new protocols that involved family life, mainly childbirth. While many resented the power that she held in the royal court, there was no doubt that she used her influence to stabilize the Tudor dynasty. While Edward IV owed much of his success to the Kingmaker, Richard Neville, Henry VII owed his kingship to his mother, who also earned the title "Kingmaker." Margaret and Elizabeth Woodville had a notoriously strained relationship, but they were able to work together to arrange Prince Arthur's marriage to the Spanish Infanta, Catherine of Aragon.

Unfortunately, Elizabeth of York died in 1503 due to complications of childbirth when she gave birth to her youngest daughter, Catherine, who also died. With the queen gone, Margaret became the most important woman in the Tudor court, and she would go on to outlive her only son and play an important role during the beginning of Henry VIII's reign.

Personality

Throughout his life, Henry VII received a lot of help that allowed him to take the English throne, but his own efforts and personality helped him to endure exile and the challenges of ruling. He had a fascinating life as the first Tudor monarch, and his efforts stabilized England after thirty years of war. According to his contemporaries, he had a good memory, which helped him with affairs of state, and he was an intelligent man with a great head for business. His approach to fines and financial punishments was a stark contrast to his predecessors' practice of battles and land grabs.

Henry's years in exile also had a lasting effect on him, as he was a cautious man who wouldn't let anyone else get too powerful during his reign. Francis Bacon praised him for being a wise man who was determined to be an independent ruler. During his lifetime, Henry VII saw rulers who suffered betrayal from their closest companions, and he was careful not to make the same mistakes. While he was known for being extremely cautious with money, he also knew the value of entertaining like a king. He threw lavish tournaments and feasts. When his son Arthur married Catherine of Aragon, he arranged a massive wedding ceremony that impressed the monarchs of Europe. As a king, he kept up appearances but didn't bankrupt himself in doing so.

Henry also took good care of his family and had a special bond with his mother. He never forgot her loyal years of service and treated her very well. As one of his trusted advisors, Margaret was allowed to propose laws and protocols that he took very seriously. He didn't view her position as his advisor as symbolic; he actively sought out her advice. While Henry was a busy king, he also took good care of his children and made time for his family. His marriage to Elizabeth of York started off as political, but he genuinely grew to love her. According to reports, he was inconsolable when she died.

Henry VII was a good king and a cautious man who didn't forget the lessons he had learned during the difficult times in his life.

Legacy

Henry VII wasn't a very popular king, as his financial policies earned him many enemies, but he managed to navigate the country through extremely difficult times and left a stable throne behind for his son. He outlived his oldest son, Arthur, but died suddenly in 1509. His son, Henry VIII, was coronated on June 24th, 1509. While Henry VII wasn't known as the greatest king in English history, he still did his best during extremely difficult times. He was buried alongside his wife at Westminster Abbey, and his building efforts at Westminster Abbey were immortalized when a chapel was named after him.

16. Henry VII Chapel at Westminster Abbey

Henry VII was born during difficult times and had an uncertain future, but he rose to incredible heights and ushered in a new dynasty that would become one of England's most famous royal families.

Chapter 5: Henry VIII (r. 1509–1547)

Henry VIII was arguably the most infamous Tudor. He started off as the second son of a king and was expected to become nothing greater than a duke. The generation before him had been subjected to a war that wiped out many noble families and who knew the danger of ambitious men who were allowed to get too close to the throne. Henry VII settled the country down after the civil war and left a stable throne for his family. His lineage was secure, and his son, Arthur, was being primed for the throne. Unfortunately, Arthur died, and Henry VII's second son was thrust into the spotlight.

17. Henry VIII

During his lifetime, Henry VIII achieved many great things. He won wars and passed successful policies, but his triumphs were overshadowed by his personal drama. When he failed to produce a legitimate heir, he went to great lengths to secure the future of the Tudor lineage, which led to several dramatic and failed marriages. Henry left the Catholic Church and set the stage for decades of religious upheaval that turned England from a Catholic to a Protestant country. He left behind a fascinating legacy that still captures the imagination of the general public.

Life as the Second Son

Henry was born in 1491 and was given several appointments while he was still a toddler, such as the Lord Warden of the Cinque Ports, Lord Lieutenant of Ireland, and Duke of York. It's likely that these positions were given to him at such a young age so that his father could keep control of the positions until his son was old enough to assume the responsibilities that were given to him. He was raised well and given the best tutors. He became fluent in French and Latin, which was expected of royal children at the time. Few records exist of his childhood since no one expected that such records would be important.

According to contemporary reports, he was an athletic youth who enjoyed participating in the tournaments that his father arranged, which he often won. He also enjoyed hunting and dancing and was reportedly an excellent student. Henry VIII took a keen interest in theology and built up an impressive knowledge about religious matters, which would become useful later in his life when he researched how to get out of his marriage to Catherine of Aragon. Historians have found that he enjoyed knightly pursuits, such as horse riding, tennis, and archery. While his brother was sickly and spent most of his time learning how to be king, Henry was allowed to pursue his own interests.

When he was a young man, he was tall and had an athletic figure, which was quite different from his later portraits that show how his excessive lifestyle had taken its toll. The intelligent young prince charmed nobles and foreign dignitaries alike, and the future of the Tudor dynasty looked bright with a studious crown prince and an enthusiastic duke of York. Unfortunately, things were about to change for the entire family, and Henry would be required to step up and learn the business of ruling a kingdom.

Prince Arthur

When Henry VII and Elizabeth of York got married, they unified the warring Houses of York and Lancaster. Their son would be the ultimate symbol of that unification, a prince who would become king and belong to both sides of the war. They likely hoped that he would have an easier time ascending the throne than Henry VII did. Arthur was born in September 1486 and was given the titles prince of Wales and earl of Chester. His parents and their advisors immediately began scouring Europe to find the perfect marriage alliance. When Arthur was eleven years old, he was betrothed to Catherine of Aragon, the daughter of the Spanish monarchs. The alliance represented the hopes that the two royal houses would become powerful allies, which would help secure both dynasties.

18. Prince Arthur Tudor

A popular belief exists that Arthur was a sickly child, but there isn't a lot of evidence to support that theory. By many accounts, Arthur was a gentle person who did well in his studies as he trained to become king. While he was still a teenager, he was sent to Wales to secure authority in the country on behalf of his father. At fifteen years old, he was married to Catherine of Aragon. His family spared no expense for the wedding ceremony that took place in September 1501, and it was apparently one of the most lavish events in English history. The wedding was a clear demonstration of the Tudors' prosperity and signified the great hopes that were invested in the marriage.

Once the royal couple was married, they were sent to Ludlow Castle. However, Arthur was growing sicker as time went on, and there are theories that he was suffering from the mysterious sweating sickness. The illness arrived on English shores when Henry VII became king, and it was a serious concern during the beginning of his reign. The sweating sickness struck quickly, and people reportedly died within hours of developing symptoms. In March 1502, Arthur and Catherine became ill during an outbreak of the sweating sickness. Catherine survived, but Arthur didn't. The Tudor dynasty was shocked by the tragedy. As news of Arthur's death spread, Henry was thrust into the spotlight, and Catherine's own future was in danger.

Political Life

When Arthur died, Henry became the heir, and his father's last years were spent training Henry to become the next king. In 1509, Henry VII died, and his son became King Henry VIII. He was eighteen years old. There were high hopes for Henry VIII's reign. He was young, handsome, charming, and athletic. His father had been unpopular because of his strict financial policies, but Henry VIII had a much different personality. Almost as soon as Henry VIII became king, he dismissed some of his father's unpopular financial policies, which endeared him to the public. Unfortunately, he soon found that it was necessary to reintroduce several of those policies since he had ambitious military plans.

Henry's court was famous for allowing men of lower birth to gain power. One such example was Thomas Wolsey. He was the son of a butcher but became the cardinal archbishop of York and one of Henry's closest advisors for some time. Another famous advisor was Thomas Cromwell, whose father was a blacksmith. For much of his reign, Henry was influenced by powerful advisors who could rise from nothing to become some of the most powerful men in the kingdom. The fortunes of these men, Cromwell and Wolsey in particular, were dependent on Henry's favor, which could prove to be fickle if he didn't get what he wanted. When Cromwell and Wolsey fell out of favor, Henry elected a Privy Council that was made up of multiple advisors instead of just one favorite.

19. Thomas Wolsey

Henry also worked with English Parliament and was intent on creating a united kingdom by becoming king of Wales and Ireland. In 1536, Wales was included in the state of England. Henry also created the Council of the North, which helped him rule the north of England more effectively. Welsh was banned, and in 1543, the country was divided into manageable counties. In 1541, Henry named himself the king of Ireland, which indicated his determination to bring Ireland more firmly under his rule.

Besides taking more control over Britain and Ireland, Henry also had dreams of foreign conquests and was eager to go to war for the glory of England.

Foreign Conquests

In 1512, Henry got his chance at military glory when he joined an alliance with Ferdinand II of Aragon against France. His advisors were unhappy about the alliance, but Henry was ready to go to war. The campaign was arranged by Wolsey, and Wolsey's support proved to cement his friendship with the king. When Henry VIII declared war on France in 1513, Scotland responded by declaring war on England. Henry set sail to invade France, while Scotland invaded England in an effort to distract Henry from his war. James IV of Scotland was eager to win independence from England, and he was France's loyal ally. James was defeated by the earl of Surrey at the Battle of Flodden, where he was killed along with many of his nobles.

In 1513, Henry had his first taste of glory when he won the Battle of the Spurs, after which he captured Thérouanne and Tournai. However, Henry was unable to keep up the invasion of France, and in 1514, his sister Mary married the French king to form an alliance between the two nations. Henry never got his glorious war with France and was forced to make a series of peace treaties with the French. During his reign, he spent a lot of time and effort creating a navy, which included massive warships.

There's no doubt that Henry VIII wanted to be a heroic warrior, but his dreams of glory on the battlefield were pushed into the background as his personal life took center stage. As king, he was required to produce a male heir who would succeed him, and his failures to do so would eventually rip England away from the Catholic Church and lead to the English Reformation. The road to reformation began with the "Great Matter" of his marriage to Catherine of Aragon.

Catherine of Aragon

Catherine of Aragon was the daughter of King Ferdinand and Queen Isabella of Spain. Her marriage to Prince Arthur was meant to secure a powerful ally for England, but when her young husband died just months after their wedding, she was left in a difficult position. The problem was seemingly solved when it was decided that Catherine would marry Henry. Unfortunately, this plan was problematic since Catherine was Arthur's widow, and such a pairing was considered incestuous. As a result, they needed papal dispensation to be allowed to marry. It took a few years, but soon after Henry was crowned, he married Catherine.

20. Catherine of Aragon

It would appear as though Henry truly loved Catherine, and the two had a very happy marriage at first. They were married for twenty-three years, and Henry trusted Catherine implicitly. When he left to invade France in 1513, he entrusted the care of the country to Catherine. However, Henry needed an heir. Although

Catherine became pregnant and gave birth a few times, only one child, Mary, survived to adulthood. As time went on, Henry became increasingly desperate for an heir. Matters worsened for Catherine in 1519 when Henry's mistress, Elizabeth Blount, gave birth to a boy who was recognized as Henry's son. He was given the title of duke of Richmond.

For years, Henry viewed Catherine as a model wife and always praised her as such, but when she failed to give him an heir, he decided to take drastic measures.

The English Reformation

When Catherine of Aragon became forty, her chances of providing Henry with a legitimate heir dwindled to nothing. The king began to think of ways to get a different wife. In the 1520s, one of the queen's ladies-in-waiting, Anne Boleyn, caught the king's eye, and he fell madly in love. He decided that she would be the perfect second wife, but the problem was that he needed to get rid of Catherine of Aragon first. Anne Boleyn was an ambitious woman, and she wasn't prepared to settle for being the king's mistress. She refused to start a family with him before marriage. King Henry VIII was stuck in a very difficult situation, which he referred to as the "Great Matter." The Catholic Church didn't permit divorce, and he didn't want to wait until Catherine died.

21. Henry VIII meets Anne Boleyn

Henry VIII had an avid interest in theology and discerned that the only way out of his marriage barring death was an annulment granted by the pope. He used the principle of the Prohibition of Leviticus to argue that his marriage to Catherine was never valid. According to Leviticus, a man was forbidden from marrying his brother's widow. Unfortunately for Henry VIII, Charles V was the emperor of the Holy Roman Empire, and he was Catherine's nephew. The pope at the time was Clement VII, and he wasn't going to risk Charles V's displeasure by granting Henry an annulment.

Faced with opposition from the papal office and most of the rulers in Europe, Henry had to get creative. In 1529, Cardinal Lorenzo Campeggio was sent to investigate the "Great Matter," but nothing was decided. Henry separated from Catherine. In the meantime, he lived with Anne Boleyn, who refused to sleep with him. However, in 1532, Anne Boleyn changed her mind, and she soon became pregnant. This increased Henry's desperation to get his marriage annulled.

Together with Wolsey, Henry concocted a creative plan to separate the church in England from the church in Rome, which would make Henry the head of the Church of England. This would give him total control of the church. Unfortunately, Wolsey wasn't able to achieve this. In 1530, Wolsey was accused of treason, which indicates how far he had fallen from the king's favor. He died while en route to his trial, but he probably would have been executed had he not died of natural causes. He was replaced by Thomas More, who refused to take the Oath of Supremacy and was promptly accused of treason and executed soon afterward. Thomas More was replaced by Thomas Cromwell.

Henry VIII's marriage was annulled by Thomas Cranmer, Archbishop of Canterbury, in 1533, and the Act of Succession was passed, which made Henry's daughter, Mary, illegitimate. Henry was excommunicated from the Catholic Church, but in 1534, the Act of Supremacy was passed. This act made Henry the highest authority in the Church of England, which meant that he, not the pope, was allowed to settle all legal matters. And finally, the Treason Act was passed in 1534, which made it treasonous to criticize the king. The Treason Act meant that Henry was allowed to execute anyone who spoke against the monarch. These people were seen as traitors, which would have violent consequences as the English Reformation progressed.

At first, Henry only wanted control of the church, but eventually, the Church of England faced serious reforms that led to England becoming a predominantly Protestant country. However, the English Reformation only started with Henry, as it would be continued by his heirs. In the meantime, Henry had a new wife and was eager to finally get a legitimate male heir. In fact, his enthusiasm for an heir was so great that Anne Boleyn's entire life was dependent on her giving birth to a boy.

Meanwhile, Catherine of Aragon never agreed to the annulment and was shocked by Henry's actions. In 1536, she died at

Kimbolton Castle with the knowledge that her daughter had been disinherited.

Anne Boleyn

Anne Boleyn was the woman who sparked the English Reformation, and she finally became queen in 1533. She had spent some of her childhood in the French court, where she learned the ways of the royal court. Her sister, Mary, had become Henry's mistress sometime in the 1520s but was eventually married off. Anne inspired a deeper sense of commitment in Henry and fought for years to be made his queen. When she became pregnant in 1533, there were high hopes that she would finally provide Henry with a male heir, but she gave birth to the future Queen Elizabeth I instead.

22. Anne Boleyn

As their relationship progressed, Henry became increasingly disillusioned with her, especially as she failed to give birth to a boy. Their relationship dissolved as the couple slipped into despair, and Henry took another mistress. Finally, Henry had Anne arrested on counts of treason and adultery. Their marriage was annulled in 1536, just two days before Anne was beheaded. While Anne didn't provide Henry VIII with an heir, she had inadvertently helped him find a way to do whatever he wanted.

Jane Seymour

As soon as Anne was dead, Henry moved on to a new wife. He married his mistress, Jane Seymour, who had served both Anne and Catherine. According to historical reports, Anne and Jane had fought on multiple occasions before Anne's death. Henry and Jane married soon after Anne was beheaded, and in 1537, Jane gave birth to Henry's heir, Edward. Jane managed to do something that neither of Henry's previous wives had done, but she didn't live long enough to enjoy her triumph.

Jane Seymour died a few weeks after giving birth to her son, and at the king's request, she was laid to rest at St. George's Chapel, where he would eventually be buried next to her.

Anne of Cleves, Catherine Howard, and Catherine Parr

Once Henry had his son, he married three more times, but he was now relieved of the burden of worrying about his heir. He married Anne of Cleves two years after Jane died in order to secure an alliance with the German duke of Cleves. Unfortunately, he was distressed by Anne's looks and divorced her in 1540, about six months after their marriage. She lived off her generous divorce settlement for the rest of her life.

23. Anne of Cleves

By 1540, Henry was no longer the young athletic king who had ruled England energetically. He was overweight and unable to walk properly due to an injury in his leg, but that didn't stop him from marrying the young and beautiful Catherine Howard. The king was infatuated with his new bride and gave her many gifts, but their differences proved to be too great. Rumors soon emerged that Catherine had been unfaithful. In 1542, Catherine Howard was executed on charges of treason and adultery.

A few months later, Henry married his final wife, Catherine Parr. Catherine was a very intelligent woman who influenced culture, education, and religion. She was reportedly a kind woman who took good care of Henry's children and stabilized Henry's personal life. Henry VIII's last wife provided him with a few years of peace as his energy dwindled and his life came to an end.

Legacy and Reputation

In his youth, Henry was an avid athlete who was crowned the victor at many of his father's tournaments. He was a handsome young man who charmed the royal court and bravely rose to the task of ruling England when his older brother died. However, in his later years, he was so overweight and sick that he had to be wheeled around. His leg was so ulcerated that it reportedly festered and stank. He died in January 1547, leaving his hard-won heir, Edward VI, to be crowned as king at only nine years old.

When Henry VIII became king at seventeen, there were high hopes for his reign. While he achieved great things, there aren't many arguments in favor of his policies and character. Henry VIII began his rule as a hopeful youth who dreamed of glory, but he would be remembered mostly for his climatic split with the Catholic Church and his melodramatic love life.

Chapter 6: Edward VI (r. 1547–1553)

Henry VIII spent most of his life agonizing about the fact that he needed an heir to continue the Tudor dynasty. He split England from the Roman Catholic Church so that he could annul his first marriage. However, he had to marry twice more before he finally fathered a legitimate son who would inherit the throne. Unfortunately, Henry VIII also led a life of excess that led to his premature death. This prevented him from helping to guide his heir. Edward VI was a young boy when he took the throne, and he was left in the care of advisors who used his power for their own gain.

24. Edward VI

While Henry VII was a relatively unpopular king, he left behind a secure throne with a decent-sized treasury. Henry VIII, on the other hand, grew to be unpopular in his later years and left behind a country that was on the brink of political instability. Thanks to his efforts, the English Reformation had begun, which opened the doors to conflict between Protestants and Catholics. That religious conflict would stir up serious issues for his heirs. Edward VI was still a child when he claimed a throne that desperately required a strong king.

Early Life

When Henry VIII turned his attention to Jane Seymour, he was still married to Anne Boleyn. He had become disillusioned with his marriage since he had expected his second wife to give birth to a son, but after a few years, their relationship deteriorated. Jane Seymour served Anne as a lady-in-waiting, and her relationship with the king often made her a target for Anne's anger. However, the king stuck by Jane's side and married her as soon as he could. Soon after they were married, Jane gave birth to Edward VI on October 12th, 1537. The birth was difficult, and Jane died a few days afterward.

His birth caused several rumors, and later on, people would claim that he had to be cut from his mother's body. When he was born, Henry arranged massive celebrations, and the whole country was delighted with the birth of the young boy. The general public also preferred Jane Seymour over Anne Boleyn, as Anne had a terrible reputation and was widely hated.

Edward grew up to be a vibrant young boy who shared his father's love of sports and music. His father made sure to provide him with good tutors, and he proved to be a good student. He learned subjects such as theology, Greek, Latin, French, military engineering, and geography. As soon as he became king, he began making records of important events, which later helped historians gain an accurate picture of his reign.

In time, Edward VI would lay the foundations that led to England turning from Catholicism to Protestantism. His efforts on behalf of the Protestant Church meant that he was widely revered by Protestants, who embellished details of his life, but the truth was that he was a bright boy who benefited from the privileges of a royal upbringing. Soon after his mother's death, his father remarried again, but Henry VIII's fourth and fifth marriages didn't last long. However, Henry VIII's final marriage provided his children with a conscientious stepmother who would have a lasting impact on the young king.

Catherine Parr

Catherine Parr had been married twice before the king met her. She had a good reputation and displayed a natural talent for avoiding the king's anger. After she married the king in 1543, she took a keen interest in her stepchildren and took care of their education. She developed a friendship with each of his children, which was likely a refreshing change of pace for the children of a king who kept changing wives.

25. Catherine Parr

During this time, the church was quickly undergoing various reforms, and some people were turning to Protestantism, which angered the Catholic clergy and led to conflict. Even the queen of England wasn't immune to this anger. When she showed an interest in Protestantism, she made powerful enemies, such as Stephen Gardiner. She was nearly imprisoned in 1546, but the king intervened on her behalf, and she was spared the humiliation.

Catherine was an intelligent woman with an excellent education. She loved learning, and she was also the first woman to publish an original English book in her own name in England. The king trusted her greatly, so when he went on a military campaign in France, he appointed Catherine as regent while he was away. And if he died, she would have been responsible for Edward until he was old enough to rule. While acting as regent, she signed royal proclamations and took care of financial matters. She didn't sit back and wait for the king to return but rather took her duties very seriously. Some historians theorize that Catherine Parr had a lasting effect on her stepdaughter, Elizabeth.

Henry deeply respected Catherine and made provisions for her before he died. He ordered that she receive the respect of a queen for the rest of her life. Soon after he died, Catherine married Thomas Seymour, the brother of Edward Seymour, who became the Lord Protector of England when Edward VI became king. She took care of Lady Elizabeth, Henry VIII's second daughter, for a short time and published another book. Edward VI held Catherine in high regard, and the two exchanged many letters. Unfortunately, Catherine Parr died in 1548 after giving birth to her first child. She was the first person to have a Protestant funeral of a royal in England. Catherine Parr was a unique woman who left a lasting impression on the Tudor heirs.

The Young King

Edward VI was crowned in January 1547, and he wasn't governed by a regent. While he was officially ruling, the Privy Council held a lot of power. They elected Edward Seymour, Edward VI's maternal uncle, as Lord Protector. Edward Seymour's position gave him unrestricted access to the king, and he became Edward VI's principal advisor. Seymour held immense power and ruled England through his young nephew. The two shared a love of military strategy and spent time studying military and naval battles. Unfortunately for Seymour, he lost favor in 1549 and was replaced by John Dudley. Edward had to deal with ambitious nobles who wanted to rule his country for him, as well as war with Scotland and strained relations with France. To make matters worse, the royal treasury was in danger, as officials had embezzled funds from the crown. The country slipped into economic instability.

The young king was also a staunch Protestant, and while the true extent of his involvement in Protestant reforms is unknown, he must have, at the very least, supported the efforts of Thomas Cranmer, who led the English Reformation in Edward VI's name. These reforms were controversial and caused real conflict that would have violent consequences. While the king faced many problems during his reign, he also had a few triumphs. In 1549, the *Book of Common Prayer* was authorized, and it became a highly influential literary work that is seen as one of the king's greatest achievements. In 1551, Edward was allowed to join the French chivalric Order of St. Michael, which reflected improved relations with France.

Despite his youth, Edward knew the importance of keeping up appearances, and his luxurious lifestyle at the royal court impressed foreign ambassadors. He was an energetic young man who enjoyed sports, hunting, and masques. The young king was also a compassionate person who showed genuine concern for his subjects by commissioning grain surveys and encouraging the cloth trade. While only a young teenager, Edward VI faced serious problems during his reign, but he did the best he could.

Edward Seymour and John Dudley

When Jane Seymour became queen, her family quickly gained political power. Her brother, Edward, became the earl of Hertford and led English forces against the Scottish and French, which earned him the king's favor. When Henry VIII died, Edward Seymour was given the post of Lord Protector by the Privy Council and became the duke of Somerset. While Seymour won military glory, he wasn't a very good politician. He tried to secure a marriage alliance for Edward VI with the Scottish princess, Mary. Unfortunately, the Scots weren't in favor of the alliance, and Seymour invaded Scotland in 1547, which further antagonized the

Scots. He tried to smooth over religious tensions with the first *Book of Common Prayer,* which aimed to provide a compromise between Catholic and Protestant beliefs. He also revoked the heresy laws passed by Henry VIII.

26. Edward Seymour, Duke of Somerset

Finally, Seymour decided to get rid of enclosures. This was the practice of using fertile land for grazing, and Seymour's decision to forbid the practice led to serious backlash from landowners. With many landowners allied against him, the final blow to his power came when the poorer classes rebelled in Norfolk. Seymour was imprisoned in 1549 and released the next year. Unfortunately, his main rival, John Dudley, had gained more power during Seymour's absence. Seymour was executed on charges of supposed treason in 1551.

With his main rival executed for treason, John Dudley could grasp royal power. He was an ambitious man who rose to the rank of duke of Northumberland. As the most powerful man on the Privy Council, he took wealth from the church and continued the English Reformation. While he mainly tried to gain more power for himself, he tried to help the English economy by expanding trade and fighting inflation. Unfortunately, he is mainly remembered for being an unscrupulous politician who only cared about his own power. His power was tied to Edward VI, and once the young king died, Dudley would try to use the Devise for the Succession to his own advantage, which had disastrous consequences.

The Reformation Continued

Edward VI was responsible for more drastic departures from Catholicism than his father. Under the archbishop of Canterbury, Thomas Cranmer, the Church of England saw serious changes during Edward VI's reign. While Henry VIII was king, the Protestant Reformation had gained massive popularity at the expense of the Catholic Church. To many, the Catholic Church had been abusing its power for too long, and it had gained too much wealth. In 1539, the state began to close down monasteries and directed the money from the monasteries to the royal treasury. This had a serious impact on English citizens since monasteries were community centers that provided medicine, financial aid, and employment.

When Edward VI became king, more drastic changes were implemented. Cranmer issued sermons that had to be used in services, and the *Book of Common Prayer* was made compulsory. Catholic teachings, such as transubstantiation and purgatory, were no longer allowed. These reforms had a real impact on the way people worshiped and were popular with some people but were viewed as heresy by others. The Bible was translated into English and widely distributed, while icons, stained glass, and murals were removed from churches. While the religious reforms were supposed to purify worship, it was also a lucrative undertaking that enriched the nobility and the royal family.

These reforms weren't implemented easily, and many Catholics protested. When the monasteries were abolished, any dissenters were executed. In an act that shocked Christendom, the abbots of Reading, Woburn, Colchester, and Glastonbury were hanged for resisting when their monasteries were shut down. The general public also revolted when their monasteries were abolished. Edward VI faced more revolts when England's economy faced problems. The decline in prosperity and changes to centuries-old traditions were too much for the people, who longed for stability. In 1549, a serious rebellion was led by Robert Kett in Norfolk but was viciously defeated by a mercenary force. The English Reformation led to unprecedented changes in the church, but it also led to terrible acts of brutality to enforce the reforms.

Instability in England

Although there was no regency when Henry VIII died, with his son becoming the king in his own right, it was apparent that the young king was ruled through his Privy Council. Edward VI was too young to know any better, and he was utterly devoted to his religion. While he had some good ideas about ruling, he was still only a child who was a few years away from reigning on his own. As a result, he was content with the reforms that were being carried out in his name since they conformed with his own religious beliefs. Unfortunately, these reforms had a serious impact on his kingdom's stability.

Meanwhile, his advisors did their best to gain as much power before the king reached an age where he felt he didn't need them anymore. The Privy Council was split under men such as Edward Seymour and John Dudley, who didn't mind causing further instability as long as it furthered their own interests. For example,

John Dudley was happy to join a coalition of landowners and Catholics who conspired against Edward Seymour, but as soon as Seymour was displaced, Dudley continued the English Reformation and secured a lucrative title for himself.

While the nobility and royal family benefited from the Protestant reforms that directed the wealth of the church into the royal treasury, the country was suffering economically. The English coin was debased, which meant the value of the English currency was quickly lowered. This had a serious effect on aspects like trade. The nobility and political officials also had no qualms about embezzling funds from the state and royal family. The royal coffers had also been dried up by Henry VIII's lavish lifestyle. The country was suffering, and as peasants became poorer and more desperate, they received little help from their political leaders and were driven to rebel. These revolts were worsened by the reformation. For centuries, the people had worshiped in the same way, and they had come to accept monasteries and Catholic practices as cornerstones of their existence.

While Edward VI's Privy Council fought each other for dominance and his people suffered through times of unprecedented changes, the king also had to deal with difficult foreign affairs.

War with Scotland

The Tudor dynasty clashed with Scotland on multiple occasions. Henry VII's daughter, Margaret, became the queen of Scotland in an effort to forge an alliance between England and Scotland. Unfortunately, peace was abandoned when Henry VIII invaded France during the early years of his reign, as Scotland invaded England in retaliation. As Henry VIII struggled to secure an heir, it looked as though his nephew, James V, would inherit the English throne. However, those hopes ended when Edward VI was born. James V died in 1542, leaving his baby daughter, Mary, to become the queen of the Scots. In 1543, the Treaty of Greenwich was signed, which ensured peace between England and Scotland and secured a marriage alliance between Mary and Edward VI.

27. Battle of Pinkie

LORD GREY OF WILTON'S CHARGE AT PINKIE (*see page* 137).

In an effort to implement the Treaty of Greenwich, Edward VI's advisor, Edward Seymour, invaded Scotland. In 1547, the two countries fought at the Battle of Pinkie. The English forces won the battle, and the day came to be known as "Black Saturday" to the Scots. Meanwhile, the young queen was smuggled out of the country to France, where she was betrothed to the French Dauphin, Francis. She married Francis in 1558 and became the queen of France when Francis ascended the throne the next year. The war against Scotland was expensive, and it was considered a failure, as Scotland and France developed a strong alliance as a result of Mary's betrothal. Unfortunately, Edward VI couldn't do much to strengthen his relationship with Scotland since he had too many problems in his own country. In time, he developed an illness that would lead to his untimely death.

Devise for the Succession

Edward VI's reign was marked by political and religious changes. He was a devout Protestant who approved of massive reforms in the church and went through a lot of effort to spread his Protestant ideals throughout his country. Unfortunately, in 1553, he caught a fever that led to a serious illness. He was only fifteen years old when he realized that he was dying. This left him with a serious problem. The young king hadn't fathered a son to continue his line, and his official heir was his half-sister, Mary. The only problem was that Mary was a staunch Catholic who was horrified by the English Reformation. As the daughter of Catherine of Aragon, she was allied with some of the most powerful Catholic monarchs in Europe and would certainly reverse all the Protestant reforms that had taken place during Edward VI's reign. At only fifteen years old, he was facing death and the reversal of his life's work. His advisors were also in trouble since their power and fortunes rested on the young king.

Instead of allowing Mary to take the throne, Edward VI began looking for ways to prevent Mary from taking the throne. Unfortunately, they couldn't exclude Mary from the line of succession since Henry VIII had recognized Mary and Elizabeth as being eligible to sit on the throne in 1544 with the Act of Succession. Besides that, if they excluded Mary, they would also have to exclude Elizabeth, who was a Protestant. Instead, Edward VI and the duke of Northumberland focused on Lady Jane Grey, the granddaughter of Edward VI's aunt. Lady Jane Grey was connected to the throne, and she was a Protestant. The duke of Northumberland quickly betrothed his son, Guildford Dudley, to Lady Jane Grey and brought his proposal before the sickly king.

Edward VI signed the Devise for the Succession, and it was quickly passed by Parliament. As the king's health declined, he invited his sister, Mary, to come to him. However, Mary had grown up in a dangerous court, and she knew better than to go to the king. Instead, she traveled to East Anglia and waited for the king to die. Finally, the young king died in July 1553, and Lady Jane Grey became the queen of England.

Legacy

For most of his life, Henry VIII went to extraordinary efforts to get a male heir to continue the Tudor line. His efforts resulted in a religiously divided country and a nine-year-old boy on the throne of England. Edward VI faced immense troubles during his short reign, but he might have been able to grow into a great king if he had lived. Instead, he died at fifteen years of age, and one of his last acts was to disinherit his older sister and put a young girl on the throne in an effort the preserve the Protestant reforms.

While Henry VIII went to great pains to secure a son, his son was ruled by ambitious men who allowed England to slip into instability to secure their own wealth. Edward VI's reign was marked by monumental changes, but the truth is that he was little more than a puppet in the hands of unscrupulous advisors. Unfortunately, the Devise of Succession would ultimately fail, and the throne would pass on to a woman who was willing to use brutality to undo the English Reformation.

Chapter 7: Mary I (r. 1553–1558)

Catherine of Aragon suffered several miscarriages, and some of her children died soon after they were born. At the time, childbirth was a difficult process; many children died before their first birthday. But as the queen of England, Catherine's losses meant national disappointment. While she never gave birth to a prince, she was able to have a daughter who would outlive her. Princess Mary had a bright future ahead of her, but when her father had his first marriage annulled, the young princess was disinherited. Her fortunes changed drastically as a result.

28. Mary I

For years, Mary had to live in obscurity since her royal birthright was denied. She was the granddaughter of some of the most powerful monarchs in Europe, but she had to watch as her mother was set aside for Anne Boleyn. Worse yet, her beloved religion was replaced by Protestantism since her younger brother was a devout Protestant. When Edward VI's health declined, Mary began making plans to take the throne of England, but once again, she was denied her birthright when Edward VI named Lady Jane Grey as his successor. However, Mary wasn't going to passively allow someone else to take her throne. In time, Mary I finally ascended to the throne, and she began putting Catholicism back in place. Unfortunately, royal life was full of more disappointments, as Mary I had to deal with the same fertility problems as her mother and faced a court full of enemies who wanted to put her younger Protestant sister on the throne.

Princess Mary

Mary was born in 1516 and was Catherine's fifth child; however, she was the only child who survived infancy. Despite Henry VIII's desire to have a son, he loved Mary deeply and often boasted about her beauty and temperament. When she was only two years old, she was betrothed to the Dauphin of France, Francis, but the marriage never took place, as their betrothal was broken a few years later. At six years old, she was betrothed to Charles V, the Holy Roman emperor, but that contract also fell through. During that time, another marriage contract was negotiated with the French, but an alliance was secured without the need for marriage, leaving the young princess once again single. Finally, it was suggested that Mary should marry James V of Scotland, but the two were never betrothed. The subject of Mary's marriage would be discussed throughout her life, but the contracts somehow always fell through. Unfortunately for the young princess, she would only marry once she was queen and far past her prime years.

While the royal court was trying to find a suitable marriage alliance for the princess, she grew up to be a well-mannered and accomplished child. She studied Latin, music, dance, French, and Spanish. When she was nine years old, she was sent to the border of Wales and given her own court at Ludlow Castle. She was called the "Princess of Wales," but there is no evidence that she was ever invested with the title, likely because the privileges were usually reserved for the crown prince, and Henry still held out hope that he could get a son.

The young princess lived a charmed life and enjoyed all the privileges of her station. She was close to her mother and shared many of Catherine of Aragon's traits. Those traits, such as her pride and stubbornness, would affect the rest of Mary's life.

The Act of Succession

Unfortunately, Catherine's barrenness would have serious effects on the young princess's life. As Mary grew from a child to a young woman, it became common knowledge that her father was dissatisfied with her mother and that he frequently took mistresses. This wasn't uncommon for the time period, and such news wasn't particularly distressing, even though it was stressful for the queen. However, everything changed when the king became obsessed with Anne Boleyn. Suddenly, Catherine had become part of the "Great Matter" that Henry wanted to solve. Catherine Aragon went from being the queen of England to an irritation that prevented Henry from getting what he wanted.

During her teen years, Mary was forced to watch from the sidelines as her father sought permission to annul his marriage to her mother, a move that would disinherit her. Pope Clement VII was stuck in a difficult position, as Charles V had surrounded Rome during the War of the League of Cognac. If he indulged Henry VIII's request, he would risk angering Charles V, who was Catherine of Aragon's nephew. The pope had enough to deal with and chose to reject Henry VIII's request for an annulment. While this may have been a relief to Catherine and Mary, it only served to push Henry VIII to take drastic action.

In time, Henry separated from the church in Rome and made himself the head of the Church of England. This was a shocking decision, which Catherine and Mary viewed as heresy. In 1533, Catherine's marriage to Henry was annulled, and in 1534, the Act of Succession was passed. This act declared that the king's marriage to Anne was "undoubted, true, sincere and perfect" and made Mary illegitimate. Catherine refused to acknowledge that her marriage was illegitimate, and for years, Mary followed her mother's example until she was finally pressured to accept the Act of Succession.

Adolescence

As Mary's parents' marriage fell apart and various marriage alliances failed to become a reality, Mary was reportedly frequently sick. To make matters worse, her mother was forced to move to obscure palaces while Henry continued life at court with Anne by his side. Mary wasn't allowed to see her mother, and the two were forced to correspond secretly. This would have added to Mary's stress since she and her mother were very close. The young princess suffered from irregular menstruation and depression, but the exact causes of her sickness aren't known. When Henry VIII married Anne and the Act of Succession was passed, Mary's household was dismissed, and she was forced to serve as her baby sister's lady-in-waiting at Hatfield. In addition, her titles were revoked, and she was called Lady Mary. Despite all the problems she faced, Mary followed her mother's example and refused to acknowledge the Act of Succession, which incensed Henry and Anne. In retaliation, her freedom was restricted, and she was often threatened. Mary got sick often and had a difficult time, especially since she still wasn't allowed to see her mother. She had few allies since her position was greatly diminished, and she had to rely on the imperial ambassador, Eustace Chapuys, to plead her case before the king.

In 1536, Catherine became ill, and Mary asked permission to travel to see her mother, but her request was denied. Catherine died shortly after, and Mary slipped into despair. During her childhood, Mary had been at the center of court life and was beloved by her father. Unfortunately, life became very difficult for her after she was stripped of her inheritance. Her relationship with her father deteriorated, and they didn't speak to each other for three years. Mary's refusal to accept the Act of Succession contributed to her troubles since the king was used to getting what he wanted. By denying Anne as the queen of England, Mary was breaking the laws that her own father had enacted.

Adulthood

In time, Anne Boleyn was executed, and a new queen took the throne. Any hope that Mary would be restored to her birthright was shattered when Edward VI was born. Jane Seymour tried to make life better for Mary and interceded with Henry on her behalf. Henry agreed to make peace with his daughter if she agreed to recognize his authority as the head of the church. Mary was pressured into accepting his demands before she was allowed to return to court. This made her life somewhat easier, as she was allowed to have a household of her own again. There were attempts to return Mary's inheritance during the English Reformation. The Pilgrimage of Grave was a rebellion led by Lord Hussey. He demanded that Mary's birthright be restored to her. Unfortunately, the rebellion was destroyed, and Hussey was executed.

Meanwhile, Mary was allowed to be her young brother's godmother, and several more marriage alliances were negotiated but fell through. At one point, she almost married the duke of Bavaria and the duke of Cleves, and there were even rumors that Thomas Cromwell tried to marry Mary. This rumor led to Cromwell's execution once the minister fell out of power. While queens came and went, Mary was allowed to live in relative peace. Following the execution of Catherine Howard in 1542, Mary was allowed to act as the hostess of the courtly Christmas Festivities, an honor that was usually reserved for the queen. Finally, Henry married Catherine Parr, who brought peace and happiness to the royal court. Henry's final queen made a real effort to be friends with the royal children. Thanks to her efforts, Mary and Elizabeth were returned to the line of succession when an updated Act of Succession was enacted in 1544. Mary was now the heir to the throne behind her younger brother, but she was legally illegitimate, which restricted her movements and privileges.

When Edward VI became ill, and it was apparent that he would die, he attempted to keep Mary from the throne since she was sure to reverse the Protestant reforms. However, Mary had spent a lifetime in one of the most dangerous courts in Europe. She wasn't going to let anyone keep her from her birthright again. Unfortunately, due to the actions of Edward VI and his Privy Council, an innocent young woman was caught in the crossfire.

Lady Jane Grey

Lady Jane Grey has become one of the most tragic figures in English history. She is known as the Nine Days' Queen and had the shortest reign in British history. Lady Jane was a young noblewoman and the daughter of the duke of Suffolk. While she was supposed to be fifth in line to the throne, Edward VI gave her precedence since she was a Protestant. John Dudley quickly identified her as the perfect heir and betrothed her to his son, Guildford Dudley. The ambitious plot was quickly approved by the dying king and his council. Lady Jane was married without delay, and on July 10th, 1553, she was crowned the queen of England. According to reports of the time, she was a beautiful young woman who had studied French, Latin, Greek, Hebrew, and Italian.

While Edward VI's Protestant reforms pervaded England, Mary refused to give up her faith and traditions. She was used to defying the orders of a king, and in 1550, she realized that her life was in danger. She almost left for mainland Europe. Edward VI's council members, John Dudley in particular, had made life very difficult for Mary. They knew that once she took the throne, she would retaliate. Efforts were made to entrap Mary in the Tower of London before Edward VI died, but Mary proved to be too shrewd for her enemies. While the Devise for the Succession was passed by Parliament, it was an unpopular plan that most of the nobility were reluctant to enforce. These two factors led to the downfall of John Dudley and Lady Jane Grey.

Mary quickly gained supporters, and on July 19th, 1553, she declared herself queen. She marched on London with a force of thirty thousand men who quickly captured Dudley, who led his own force of two thousand men. The unscrupulous duke was executed on August 22nd, 1553.

To her credit, Mary was reluctant to execute the young woman. Lady Jane Grey hadn't wanted to be queen and was pressured into the coup by her father and father-in-law. Mary was able to take the throne with little trouble, and crowds of people cheered for her in London. Unfortunately, a rebellion was raised by Sir Thomas Wyatt in 1554, and it became apparent that as long as Lady Jane Grey was alive, she would be the focus of rebellions against Mary. On February 12th, 1554, Lady Jane Grey and her husband were executed.

29. The execution of Lady Jane Grey

Philip II of Spain

When Mary became queen, crowds of people cheered for her, and most of the nobility joined her army against John Dudley's coup. Unfortunately, she wouldn't remain popular. Her determination to return England to the church in Rome would lead to disastrous consequences. Mary was crowned in 1553 and immediately began reversing the Protestant reforms, which made her unpopular among the noble classes, as they had benefited greatly from them. Most of the populace was indifferent to the reforms, but the return to Catholicism meant more instability for the country.

Mary's popularity was further damaged when she announced her betrothal to Philip II of Spain. This was an immensely unpopular decision since Spain was seen as England's enemy. Her decisions made her people suspicious, as they feared that Spain would invade England. In 1554, Sir Thomas Wyatt led a rebellious force to London, where he planned to replace Mary with her sister, Elizabeth. The rebellion was quickly defeated, and Elizabeth was placed in the Tower of London. Mary swore to her people that her loyalty would always remain with England. Parliament took its time accepting Mary's betrothal and set limits on Philip's power. He would only be allowed to act as the queen's consort, and no foreigners would be allowed to gain political positions in the country.

30. Philip II of Spain

Mary was finally married on July 25ᵗʰ, 1554, at thirty-seven years old. Unfortunately, Philip was nearly eleven years younger than Mary, and the couple spent most of their time apart. Mary announced two pregnancies, one in 1554 and one in 1557. Both turned out to be false pregnancies, and it was clear that Mary was past her childbearing years. In 1556, Philip became the king of Spain, which made Mary the queen consort of the Spanish king.

Together, they waged war on the Protestant Reformation, an action that would earn Mary the title of "Bloody Mary."

Religious and Foreign Policies

Along with her husband, Mary waged war against France in 1557. At first, the couple won a victory at Saint-Quentin, but their lack of funds led them to begin losing the war they had started. In 1558, Mary lost Calais, which had been held by England for centuries. While the war was a disaster, Mary managed to help stabilize the economy in England. Her marriage to Philip brought Spanish money to the English economy, and she governed the country well. Like her successful predecessors, Mary created specialized councils that took care of various aspects of the government. This allowed her to control the way her country was governed. Mary had spent years on the fringes of her father's court and had time to study how to do her job correctly.

Mary's main ambition was to return England to the papacy, and she enacted several Acts of Repeals to undo the English Reformation. The Second Act of Repeal in 1555 made the pope the head of the Church of England. Mary was finally able to repeal the acts that had ruined her life and allowed her religion to be reformed. Unfortunately, the queen wasn't content with merely enacting repeals; she zealously enforced her acts and began persecuting Protestants. During the next four years, she burned around 287 Protestants at the stake. These numbers included prominent men, such as Hugh Latimer, Nicholas Ridley, and Thomas Cranmer. The queen was already becoming unpopular before these acts, so the public burnings only turned the tide of public opinion against her.

However, it should be noted that Mary's acts were exaggerated to ruin her reputation. The infamous burnings were rare, and she only used the tactic as a last resort against rebellions and resistance. In fact, Mary preferred to educate the general public about religious matters and took a keen interest in how the clergy was educated.

Training schools were established, and the priesthood had detailed outlines of what was expected of them. While she did persecute Protestants, many atrocities committed against Protestants were perpetrated by angry mobs and Catholic parishioners. While Mary's actions were unsavory, it would be unfair to dismiss her completely.

Mary's time as queen was extremely stressful, as she had to deal with personal and political turmoil. She frequently had to fight with Parliament and the House of Commons, and her enemies made her job very difficult. In time, her health began to fail, and England prepared itself for a new queen.

Legacy

In 1558, Mary died from stomach cancer at the age of forty-two. At that point, she was so unpopular that the date of her death was celebrated as a public holiday for years after she died. People were relieved that the religious turmoil was over. Mary's younger sister, Elizabeth, became queen. She would face threats from Spain and her own council. Like Mary, Elizabeth had grown up in the dangerous Tudor court and had learned how to take care of herself. Elizabeth would usher in a golden age in English history, which included the English Renaissance that saw famous playwrights and poets flourish.

When Mary was born, she had a bright future as the daughter of Henry VIII and Catherine of Aragon. She led a charmed life as the princess of England, and her early proposed marriage alliances represented great hopes for her future. Unfortunately, Henry VIII betrayed his daughter in his quest for a son, and Mary was forced to live on the outskirts of a court that had once doted on her. She was forced to live through extremely difficult times but maintained her poise and dignity. Her pride and devotion to her religion moved her to defy kings and fight for what she thought was right. Mary faced threats of execution and was forced to deny her own convictions, which took a toll on her. Due to her father's actions, she remained lonely and unmarried for most of her life. The crisis of succession meant that her country was divided and unstable when she took the throne. During her time as queen, she was forced to fight for what she believed in, and in time, she died of a terrible disease, with her people celebrating her death.

Chapter 8: Elizabeth I (r. 1558–1603)

Elizabeth I is one of the most famous queens in history. She wasn't supposed to become queen; in fact, her father had disinherited her when she was still a young child. For most of her life, she was branded as the illegitimate daughter of Henry VIII and his most notorious wife, Anne Boleyn. Elizabeth's early life was tumultuous, but she survived her siblings and became the most powerful woman in England.

31. Elizabeth I

Once she became queen, the foremost issue on everyone's mind was that of her marriage. Mary I had proven that the wrong marriage could cause serious problems for the whole country, and if Elizabeth I married a foreign man, then that man could claim the right to become the king of England. However, Elizabeth I was a shrewd and forward-thinking woman who knew that the only way to keep control of her throne was by remaining single.

Elizabeth I had seen how Edward VI had been ruled by his advisors and how Mary I had to defend her throne when she married a Spanish prince. She survived the scandal of remaining unmarried and brought political, religious, and economic stability to her country. During her long reign, the arts flourished. By remaining unmarried, Elizabeth I brought an end to the Tudor dynasty. But after spending her formative years at the hands of the Tudor court, Elizabeth I was well aware of the consequences of her decision and became the "Virgin Queen."

Early Life

Anne Boleyn gave birth to Elizabeth in 1533 and named her daughter after Henry VIII's mother, Elizabeth of York. Unfortunately, Elizabeth was still a toddler when Henry VIII had his marriage to Anne annulled and branded Elizabeth as illegitimate. While Mary I spent most of her childhood as the princess of England, Elizabeth spent most of her childhood as Henry VIII's illegitimate daughter. When she was born, Henry VIII was sorely disappointed since he had pinned all his hopes on Anne giving him a son. Their marriage began to fall apart shortly after.

Henry VIII married Jane Seymour just a few days after Anne was executed, and Elizabeth faded into the background. Her early education included studying French, Dutch, Spanish, and Italian. Elizabeth showed a natural gift for learning languages, and by the time she was twelve years old, she had translated Catherine Parr's book, *Prayers or Meditations*, into Italian, French, and Latin from English, which she then gave to her father as a New Year's gift. She made a habit of translating classical works and seemed to have enjoyed the practice. Later, she studied Scottish, the Irish languages, Cornish, and Welsh. Elizabeth was a gifted student, and her final stepmother, Catherine Parr, took a keen interest in Elizabeth's education. As a result, Elizabeth studied subjects such as history, music, philosophy, rhetoric, and theology, which would later help her during her reign.

32. A portrait of Elizabeth Tudor (far right) with her father, his court jester, and her siblings

When her father died, Elizabeth lived with Catherine Parr and Thomas Seymour at their estate in Chelsea. Unfortunately, this period in her life would lead to a scandal involving Thomas Seymour. According to reports, Thomas Seymour enjoyed entering Elizabeth's rooms while he was in his nightgown and engaged in horseplay with the young teenager that involved tickling. Elizabeth didn't seem to invite these visits and went through pains to make sure that she was never alone with him. In 1548, Elizabeth left her stepmother's house after Catherine Parr allegedly discovered her husband and stepdaughter in an embrace. When Catherine Parr died a few months later, Thomas Seymour expressed a desire to marry Elizabeth. In 1549, Seymour was arrested after conspiring to marry Elizabeth after deposing his brother as Lord Protector. Elizabeth was interrogated during this time, but she never admitted to being involved in the plot. Thomas Seymour was executed on March 20th, 1549.

Thomas Wyatt's Rebellion

In 1554, a massive rebellion led by Sir Thomas Wyatt the Younger took place in opposition to Mary I's marriage to Philip II of Spain. In all fairness, the causes of the rebellion were much more intricate than the matter of the queen's marriage to a foreign prince. The English economy had been stalling ever since Henry VIII's reign, and it had been worsened by the greedy nobles who ruled through Edward VI. Several nobles also took part in the rebellion, but this was likely to increase their own wealth. When Mary I took the throne, she immediately began reversing the Protestant reforms put in place by her predecessor. However, many Protestants wanted England to become a Protestant country. All of these causes contributed to the rebellion, and when Queen Mary I announced her betrothal to Prince Philip, the rebels found a golden opportunity.

Spain was becoming rich from the loot that came from the New World, and it was a staunchly Catholic country. Rumors flourished, as nationalistic English citizens feared that the foreign prince would one day become the king of England and rob the country of its resources to build his own empire. Suddenly, the same people who had cheered for Mary I when she took the throne were murmuring against her and remembering the fact that her mother had also been Spanish. It also seemed that a few of the rebels wanted to replace Mary I with her younger sister, Elizabeth. This would have prevented the country's return to Catholicism, which would have allowed many nobles to keep the riches that they had taken from the church during the English Reformation.

The rebels planned to march in November of 1553 and planned four other uprisings that would be supported by the French, who would send their fleet to England. Word got out about the rebellion, and three of the uprisings couldn't take place. In January 1554, Wyatt led his rebel force from Kent to London in an attempt to stop the queen's marriage. At first, the rebels gained the upper hand, as they forced the royal army to retreat, and some royal soldiers joined Wyatt's cause. The rebels marched forward, and it seemed that nothing would be able to stop them. Matters looked so desperate for Mary that she was forced to destroy the bridges that crossed the River Thames.

Eventually, Thomas Wyatt reached London, where he crossed the Thames and rebuilt the bridges so that his army could enter the city. The two armies fought within London, and Wyatt was eventually surrounded. Once the rebellion was destroyed, Mary executed Wyatt and two hundred of his men. Mary was forced to execute Lady Jane Grey since she knew that the young noblewoman would be the figurehead for future rebellions. Parliament was allowed to reduce her husband's future privileges, and Elizabeth was imprisoned. Unfortunately, the rebellion served to make Mary I more paranoid, and she began persecuting the Protestants relentlessly.

The Virgin Queen

After the Wyatt rebellion was defeated in 1554, Elizabeth was imprisoned in the Tower of London, even though she had never said anything against her sister or spoken publicly about Mary's policies. After two months, Elizabeth was put under house arrest in Oxfordshire. Finally, Elizabeth made peace with her sister after a year of imprisonment and was allowed to live freely again. In 1558, Mary I died of stomach cancer, and Elizabeth was crowned at twenty-five years of age at Westminster Abbey. While her coronation was a magnificent affair, the truth was that England was in a delicate state. There were no more lands in France, and foreign alliances were far and few between. To make matters worse, the state was in serious financial straits. It was clear that everyone expected Elizabeth to marry someone as quickly as possible, and she became the most sought-after woman in the world. England needed a strong leader, and everyone expected Elizabeth's husband to be the leader they needed.

33. Elizabeth I in her coronation robes

However, instead of looking for a husband, Elizabeth began looking for capable advisors. She appointed William Cecil as her secretary, Sir Francis Walsingham as the secretary of state, and Robert Dudley the earl of Leicester. These men became Elizabeth's favorites and aided her through much of her reign. She put herself in charge of policymaking, and nobles had to approach her directly to push their ideas. The queen proved to be an independent woman who carefully took care of the royal treasury and didn't waste time on expensive foreign conquests. She took time to tour her country, and whenever anyone brought up the subject of her marriage, she claimed to be married to England. When Elizabeth I took the throne, she was courted by many nobles and received offers of marriage from Philip II of Spain, the king of Sweden, two Habsburg dukes, and a French prince.

Elizabeth used symbols that were associated with the Virgin Mary to enhance her own image as the Virgin Queen, but there were several friendships with young men that may have been intimate in nature. These friends included Sir Walter Raleigh, Sir Christopher

Hatton, and Robert Devereux, although no one held as much sway over the young queen as Robert Dudley.

Robert Dudley

Robert Dudley was born in 1532. He was the son of the duke of Northumberland, John Dudley. Unfortunately, John's father had been involved in the plot to place Lady Jane Grey on the throne and had been executed by Mary I. Robert himself had also been part of that plot and was imprisoned in the Tower of London, but Mary eventually released him. The Dudleys had been an unlucky family in regards to treason, as Robert's grandfather had also been executed for treason in 1510. Unlike Robert's family members, he was able to survive his charge of treason and became an important political figure in Elizabeth I's royal court.

34. Robert Dudley

Robert married Amy Robsart in 1550 and was appointed as the Master of the Horse. This allowed him to take care of the royal stables and transportation. He was also invited to join the highly prestigious Order of the Garter. There were reports that he and Elizabeth became friends before she ascended the throne, but there's no doubt that the two shared a close relationship by the time she became queen. Robert was given apartments close to Elizabeth's own royal rooms, and there were rumors that Robert would become Elizabeth's husband. Unfortunately for Robert, he was already married to a sickly wife. In 1560, Robert's wife fell down the stairs in the couple's home, breaking her neck and dying. Rumors began to swirl that Robert was responsible. The scandal surrounding his wife's death counted against him in the race for Elizabeth's hand. She might have sensed that she would lose the public's respect if she married Robert due to the accusations of murder and the fact that his family name had been disgraced by the charges of treason.

While Robert never became Elizabeth's husband, he was appointed as part of her Privy Council, and he became the earl of Leicester. When Mary, Queen of Scots, became a problem, Elizabeth suggested that Robert Dudley marry her, but he wisely refused. Robert was clearly the queen's favorite and hosted her frequently at his many estates, which led to her giving him more honors and lands. In time, Robert Dudley slowly fell out of favor, as the queen was distracted by other favorites. In 1578, she found out that he had married Lettice Knollys in secret, and she banished him from her court. He was allowed to return eventually and lead a force of men to support a rebellion in the Netherlands against Philip II of Spain, although his force ultimately failed. In 1588, Queen Elizabeth faced the Spanish Armada, but Robert was too sick to help his beloved queen and died that year.

Religious Policies

When Mary I took the throne, she immediately reversed many of her brother's Protestant reforms, but when it became apparent that she was going to die without an heir, the whole country braced itself for a return to Protestantism. Elizabeth I reinstated the Protestant reforms and brought the Act of Supremacy back, which made her the head of the Church of England. She also brought back the *Book of Common Prayer*. However, unlike her predecessors, Elizabeth wasn't interested in imposing her beliefs on the general public and allowed people to worship as they wished. Her policy of religious tolerance catered to the common populace, who were indifferent to royal protocols but were impacted by the religious back and forth.

Elizabeth I allowed Catholics to worship in peace, but she was excommunicated by the pope in 1570. She actively supported Protestantism and sent support to the Huguenots in France and the Protestants in the Netherlands. When she tried to impose Protestantism in Ireland, she was met with fierce backlash and multiple rebellions, which were supported by Philip II of Spain. Her policy of religious tolerance brought peace to a country that had seen many religious conflicts, but there were many who were unsatisfied with her approach and wanted to further their own agendas. The Catholics viewed Elizabeth as illegitimate since Henry VIII never received papal approval to annul his marriage to Catherine of Aragon. As a result, the Catholics began looking for a different queen.

They soon found the perfect candidate in Mary, Queen of Scots. Mary was firmly Catholic and had been brought up in France. She also had a claim to the English throne. As a result, she became the figurehead of treasonous Catholic plots against Elizabeth I.

Mary, Queen of Scots

Mary was born in 1542 and made the queen of Scotland just days after her birth when her father, James V, died. Unfortunately, she wasn't able to spend much time in her native Scotland, as the war against England forced her to flee to France, where she was betrothed to the Dauphin of France, Francis. The war against England was a result of the efforts of Henry VIII to betroth his son, Edward VI, to Mary. As the granddaughter of Margaret Tudor, Mary had a connection to the English throne, and Henry VIII hoped to unite the two countries through marriage, but the Scottish Parliament refused the betrothal.

In France, Mary was treated like a queen and given an excellent education. She was popular in the French court and known for being a lively young woman who enjoyed dancing. During her time in France, she became a Catholic, which would eventually cause serious consequences. She married Prince Francis in 1558 and became the queen of France the next year. Mary also made her claim to the English throne known, and when she returned to Scotland after Francis's death in 1560, she continued her claim. This caused problems between her and Elizabeth I. When Mary returned to Scotland, she wasn't given safe passage back home by Elizabeth. Mary refused to recognize the Treaty of Edinburgh, which accepted Elizabeth's absolute claim to the English throne.

When Mary returned to Scotland, she found that most of the country was Protestant. Many of her nobles didn't want a Catholic woman on the throne. Mary married Lord Darnley in 1565, who eventually murdered her Italian secretary, David Rizzio. Lord Darnley was murdered in 1567 but not before Mary and Darnley had a son, James Stuart. Soon after Darnley's murder, Mary married Lord Bothwell, which proved to be too much for the Scottish lords. Mary was defeated on the battlefield and imprisoned soon after. She was forced to abdicate the throne in 1567, and her son became James VI of Scotland. James VI was ruled by his lords and became a Protestant.

Mary escaped Scotland in 1568 and fled to England. Elizabeth found herself in a difficult position, and she decided to imprison Mary in different castles. In the end, Mary was imprisoned for twenty years and never saw Scotland or her son again. During the next two decades, Mary was the figurehead for several plots against Elizabeth, and in 1586, Lord Walsingham found undeniable proof of treason against Mary. Elizabeth didn't want to sign Mary's death warrant, but in 1587, Elizabeth relented. Mary was executed soon after.

Legacy

Later, Elizabeth would be accredited with fostering the best part of the English Renaissance and defeating the Spanish Armada. These were impressive feats, and Elizabeth's reign was known for being peaceful and bringing stability to England. When she became queen, she inherited a kingdom that had been drained of money and had experienced severe religious conflict. However, she soon nursed the country back to health and allowed her subjects to worship as they wished. Her triumph against the Spanish Armada would prove to be one of the most glorious Tudor victories and earn her the title Elizabeth Gloriana.

Elizabeth's decision to remain unmarried took remarkable strength of character, and it proved to be a clever choice since she never had to share her throne with anyone. Her fierce independence led to one of the most peaceful periods in English history. Despite her religious tolerance and shrewd ruling style, she still had many enemies. During her long reign, she faced treasonous plots and threats from powerful foreign kings but managed to hold her own and keep her crown. She never had any children, and when she died, the Tudor line ended with her.

While Elizabeth's reign was mostly successful, the last years of her life were defined by high taxes, inflation, and failing crops. She passed many laws and policies to help the poor, but times were tough, and there were a few food riots. Queen Elizabeth I died in 1603, and the throne passed to her closest living male relative, James VI of Scotland, who became James I of England. James I was England's first Stuart king, and the Stuarts would rule England until 1714.

The Tudor dynasty was defined by times of momentous change that saw the country split from the Church of England, as well as some of the most interesting battles of the time. Under the Tudor reign, military and warfare in England were forever changed.

Part Three: Military and Warfare

Chapter 9: Wars and Battles

The Tudor era saw some of the most important battles and wars in European history. During this time, many European countries were locked in a battle of wills that saw mighty dynasties rise and fall. The Tudors' own rise to power was aided by a bloody civil war that pitted families against each other. When Henry Tudor became king, England's army wielded medieval weapons, and men were called to arms whenever their lords summoned them. Over the next few decades, the army would be refined into a deadly force supported by superior weapons, warships, and gun forts. After all, England faced threats from France, Spain, and Scotland.

The evolution of the Tudor army can be seen through some of the most significant battles of their time. In the beginning years of the Tudors' reign, the Tudor army was armed with traditional weapons. The guns were owned and used by mercenaries. However, by the time Henry VIII went to war against France, he had powerful weapons at his disposal. Under the Tudor rule, English warfare and weapons would never be the same.

The First Battle of St. Albans, 1455

The first battle of the Wars of the Roses was far from the glorious battles that were romanticized by medieval chivalric literature. At that time, the Hundred Years' War had come to an end, and many soldiers who had fought in France were finally back home and could be called upon by their lords. The First Battle of St. Albans was fought in the streets and lanes of the town, which meant that soldiers had to fight on foot and try to get at their enemies over street barricades. It was a messy affair that would set the tone for the rest of the war.

Soldiers were armed with swords and shields, and while artillery and firearms were available, they were still difficult and unreliable. Besides that, those types of weapons were completely unsuited for the close-quarter combat that took place during the First Battle of St. Albans. The battle began on May 22nd, 1455, when Richard, Duke of York, met Henry VI. The duke of York was supported by the earl of Salisbury and the earl of Warwick, while Henry VI fought alongside the dukes of Somerset and Buckingham.

Unfortunately for Henry VI, he was outnumbered when the Yorkist alliance mustered three thousand men; he only had two thousand men at his command. To make matters worse, the Yorkist army had a force of experienced longbowmen who were led by Sir Robert Ogle, who had fought in France. The king's forces were ultimately defeated, and he was imprisoned by the Yorkists.

Battle of Bosworth, 1485

After three decades of near-constant war, England was on the brink of the final major battle of the Wars of the Roses. By that time, many noble families had become extinct, as men were executed for treason or died in battle. As various forces amassed at Bosworth Field, the stage was set for the dramatic showdown between Richard III and Henry Tudor.

On August 7th, 1485, Henry Tudor landed in Wales. As he marched, he began gathering support, and Richard was forced to meet Henry's army. Lord Thomas Stanley, Margaret Beaufort's husband, and William Stanley arrived at the battlefield with significant forces but refused to join the war until they knew who would win. Henry's army was outnumbered, but Henry had experienced allies on his side, such as the earl of Oxford. Richard commanded the duke of Norfolk to make up the vanguard, which steadily began losing against the earl of Oxford. Richard desperately commanded the duke of Northumberland to assist his army, but Northumberland didn't respond. Richard felt the need to charge at Henry himself, at which point the Stanleys joined the fray and attacked Richard III.

It was a decisive battle that saw the birth of the House of Tudor. The Yorkist forces may have numbered up to twelve thousand men and had a force of archers and a cannon. Meanwhile, Henry had about eight thousand men, with mercenaries and exiles in his ranks that had been joined by Englishmen as his army marched. The nobles and commanders in both armies fought on top of horses and wielded swords, shields, and lances, while common soldiers fought on foot. The soldiers fought with pole weapons, such as halberds, pikes, and swords.

Battle of Stoke Field, 1487

While the Battle of Bosworth Field determined that Henry VII would be the king of England, there were still many Yorkist enemies who wanted to take the throne from him. The Battle of Stoke Field took place on June 16th, 1487. In an effort to take the throne from Henry VII, the earl of Lincoln hired an army of mercenaries from Switzerland, Germany, and Ireland. Lincoln claimed to have Edward of Warwick in his possession and crowned the boy King Edward VI of England. The Yorkist army had about eight thousand men and decided that they had the advantage. They marched on England.

King Henry VII's army, once again led by the earl of Oxford, met the Yorkist army at Stoke Field. This time, Henry was in the majority with about twelve thousand men. With the River Trent behind them, the Yorkist army had no option but to fight for their lives since retreat simply wasn't possible. Despite their sincere efforts, the royal army broke their ranks and chased the mercenaries down the ravine, which became known as the Bloody Gutter. The fleeing mercenaries were cut down, and the king's army was victorious. It was soon discovered that the supposed King Edward VI was no more than a pretender, a lowborn boy known as Lambert Simnel, who was later sent to work in the king's kitchens.

Instead of executing all the traitors, Henry VII chose to impose fines on some of the leading nobles and had the Irish clergy who supported Lincoln excommunicated from the church. Lincoln chose to hire many Irish kerns, who were soldiers who could travel quickly because they were lightly armed. This may have led to Lincoln's downfall since Henry VII made sure that his army was well equipped when he marched to defeat the pretender.

Battle of Flodden, 1513

The next significant battle in the Tudor era involved Henry VIII and the king of Scotland, James IV. In 1511, Henry VII joined the Holy League alongside Spain, the pope, Venice, and the Holy Roman Empire against France. Since Scotland and France were allies, James IV was forced to negotiate with England. He offered peace on the condition that Henry VIII refrain from fighting against France, but Henry VIII rejected the offer.

35. The Battle of Flodden

THE BATTLE OF FLODDEN (see page 125).

In 1513, Henry VIII invaded France with a massive army, and James IV invaded England, taking many of his nobles with him. James IV expected that no one would be left to defend England in Henry VIII's absence and amassed a large and well-equipped army. Unfortunately for James IV, Henry had left England under the watchful care of the earl of Surrey.

Both sides were equipped with cannons, but they were difficult to transport and very slow. The Scots were mostly armed with swords, but before the battle, they had been equipped with long pikes that had been brought over by French dignitaries. This proved to be a mistake, as the Scots weren't trained to use the weapon, which was about five yards long. The long pikes were very effective when soldiers used them in unison, but the Scots hadn't had time to learn to do that yet. Thus, the weapons, which had lethal potential, were worse than useless to the Scots.

Meanwhile, the English brought many longbowmen, who fired on the Scots with deadly accuracy. Finally, the Scots were defeated, and King James IV was killed in battle along with many of his nobles, which threw Scotland into a massive crisis.

Battle of the Spurs, 1513

When Henry VIII became king, he was young and energetic with dreams of military glory. He had the royal treasury at his disposal and was surrounded by young and ambitious men who wanted their shot at battle. Finally, the perfect opportunity presented itself when Henry joined the Holy League. Not only was Henry VIII going to fight against the hated French, but he also had the backing of the papacy, which made it a holy war. Unfortunately, the war in France proved to be a difficult and expensive endeavor. In 1512, Thomas Grey failed to win Aquitaine and was forced to go back home empty-handed. In May 1513, English forces landed in Calais and immediately began marching toward Thérouanne. Henry VIII landed in Calais in June of that same year with a significant force. The army was comprised of cavalry, artillery, infantry, and longbowmen, all ready for war. They were also accompanied by hundreds of hired mercenaries.

The English army set siege to Thérouanne, while Henry VIII set up camp at a distance. In August, Holy Roman Emperor Maximilian traveled with a light force to meet Henry VIII, but Henry VIII refused to be distracted from his main goal. The French tried to break the siege but were unsuccessful, and Henry was forced to move to Guinegate. The two armies met later in August in battle, where the French hoped to engage the army and then retreat as a diversion so that supplies could be delivered to Thérouanne. Unfortunately, the plan was a disaster, as the French were attacked while retreating. They were completely defeated. Finally, Henry VIII experienced his long-awaited military glory. In time, the battle came to be known as the Battle of the Spurs, owing to how quickly the French left the battlefield on horseback.

Battle of Solway Moss, 1542

While Henry VIII hoped to bring military glory to England, he was mostly known for his infamous break with the church in Rome. When he split from the church, he advised his nephew, James V, the king of Scotland, to do the same. James V ignored his uncle's advice, and in 1542, Henry VIII sent an army to raid Scotland in retaliation. Unfortunately, the Scottish army was small and relatively unorganized.

James V responded to the English raid by sending about eighteen thousand Scots into England under Lord Maxwell. Unfortunately, the chain of command wasn't very clear, as Oliver Sinclair, one of James V's favorites, announced that he was supposed to lead the attack. The Scottish lords fought amongst themselves, which may have led to their disastrous defeat. The two armies met at Solway Moss. The English force of about three thousand men was led by Lord Wharton and Sir William Musgrave.

The battle took place near a river and marshy lands, which made it difficult to fight back or flee. According to reports, the fighting was intense, and the Scots fought with all their might but were eventually forced to retreat. Hundreds of Scottish soldiers were said to have drowned in the river. When news of the defeat reached James V, he became sick with fever and retreated to Falkland Palace, where he died at thirty years of age.

Sieges of Boulogne, 1544

In 1541, King Henry VIII was shocked to discover that his fifth wife, Catherine Howard, had been unfaithful to him. He threatened to kill her himself but was held back by his courtiers. In an effort to distract the world from his public humiliation, Henry VIII decided to declare war on France, as France was fighting with Spain over control of parts of Italy. The war would force France to renew pension payments to Henry.

Henry VIII surprisingly decided to lead the army himself, and he was joined by the duke of Norfolk and the duke of Suffolk. In 1544, Holy Roman Emperor Charles V and Henry became allies against France. The two rulers planned to lead a major force against France and capture Paris. The duke of Norfolk landed in Calais first and besieged the town of Montreuil. The siege was beset by food shortages, bad weather, and bad planning.

Henry finally left England in July 1544 with great fanfare. Instead of going to help Norfolk at Montreuil, Henry marched for Boulogne. The English forces were supported by archers, pikemen, gunners, and horsemen. Henry's siege guns were impressive and caused serious damage to Boulogne's walls. Henry was confident that he would soon defeat Boulogne. Unfortunately for Henry, he was soon bogged down by bad weather, which destroyed valuable gunpowder. Henry was only able to continue the assault on Boulogne's walls in August. In September, Boulogne surrendered, while things went badly at Montreuil.

Unfortunately, Charles V made peace with France soon after, and Henry VIII decided to go home. The battle also prompted retaliation from France, which tried to invade England through the English Channel. Henry VIII was forced to go on the defensive. In 1546, Henry VIII made peace with France and died shortly thereafter.

Battle of the Solent, 1545

In May 1545, the French brought their fleet to England in an attempt to invade the country through Portsmouth, which happened to be Henry VIII's naval base. King Henry VIII was forced to go to Portsmouth with his Privy Council to prevent the invasion. In July, the French entered the Solent with 150 warships and galleys and about 30,000 troops. The English fleet was outnumbered since they only had about eighty ships, led by the warships the *Mary Rose* and *Great Harry*. Thankfully, the English row barges were able to force the French to retreat.

Once the French were beaten back by the English navy, they decided to invade the Isle of Wight, which had a small population of well-trained civilians. They had learned to defend themselves during the Hundred Years' War. The battle dragged on, and the great warship *Mary Rose* sank during the battle. Despite this, the French were forced to retreat back to France on July 28th.

Battle of Ancrum Moor, 1545

After the Battle of Flodden, Scotland was unable to fight any wars against the English, as the country had been seriously destabilized by the resounding loss. However, the country recovered just in time to fight against England at the Battle of Solway Moss, which resulted in another major loss and the eventual death of Scotland's young king, James V. Unfortunately, James V hadn't had a male heir yet, so he left the kingdom to his infant daughter, Mary.

Henry VIII seized the chance to enforce a peace treaty with Scotland and tried to force Scotland to agree to the betrothal of Mary, Queen of Scots, to his young son, Edward. The Sots refused, which led to a series of military engagements that came to be known as the "Rough Wooing."

In 1545, an English force of about five thousand men entered Scotland, where they plundered Melrose. The Scots raised a small army in response, which was led by the earl of Angus. The Scots drew the English into a trap at sunset, which caused the English army to fall into chaos, as they were caught off guard and blinded by the bright sun. The Scots also used long pikes, which helped them win the fight, unlike at the Battle of Flodden. The English were defeated and forced to retreat.

Battle of Pinkie, 1547

Unfortunately, the Battle of Ancrum Moor wasn't the end of the Rough Wooing. When Henry VIII died, the duke of Somerset was left in charge of the young King Edward. In 1547, he planned an invasion into Scotland to conquer large portions of land. Somerset planned to use the English army and navy to his advantage, but he was met by the earl of Arran. The Scottish forces were largely outgunned and outnumbered, but their pikemen were able to inflict serious damage before the army came under fire from the English ships, artillerymen, and archers.

The Scots were forced to retreat while under heavy fire, and many drowned while trying to cross the Roman Bridge over the Esk River. While they fought bravely, the Scots were soundly defeated in the disastrous battle but were able to smuggle Queen Mary out of the country to France. Without a marriage alliance, the cost of war against Scotland was too much to justify, and England was forced to abandon the endeavor.

Loss of Calais, 1558

For hundreds of years, England and France had been enemies, as they both fought over the lands that had once been occupied by Henry II and Eleanor of Aquitaine. While most of those lands had been lost to the English, they managed to keep a strong grip on Calais. Unfortunately, in 1558, Mary I waged war on France at the urging of her husband, Philip II of Spain.

The French were provoked to engage in the fight, and the famous port town was captured by François de Lorraine in only six days. This was a tremendous loss, as Calais was a wool production center and opened up trade for staples such as lace, wool, and lead. The loss of Calais was the final straw for Mary I in her short and unsuccessful reign, and she died a few months after.

The Spanish Armada, 1588

One of the biggest challenges Elizabeth I faced during her reign came during the latter half of her rule when she was forced to face the formidable Spanish Armada. In July 1588, the Spanish Armada sailed toward England to remove its Protestant queen from the throne. For decades, the Spanish had become rich by sending ships to the New World and plundering its wealth, which allowed them to build massive warships. Elizabeth I had been a thorn in the Spanish fleet's side, as she allowed her privateers to attack and plunder Spanish ships. Finally, things deteriorated between England and Spain when Elizabeth provided aid to Protestants in the Netherlands when they rebelled against Spain.

36. The Spanish Armada

Philip II gained papal approval for his invasion and declared that his daughter, Isabella, would be the next queen of England. The Spanish soon sailed for England in their trademark crescent shape, with massive warships in the middle surrounded by smaller fighting ships. Along the way, Philip appointed the duke of Medina Sidonia to command the Spanish Armada, which turned out to be a bad decision. The duke had no seafaring experience and was frequently seasick.

Elizabeth I made Lord Howard of Effingham the commander of her fleet, and the two fleets met and began to attack each other. Drake fired on the ships from a distance, which caused the Spanish to fire back and waste their ammunition. They were forced to dock at Calais and wait for supplies. In response, the English released old ships loaded with materials that would burn up easily among the Spanish Armada. The Spanish knew that these ships could take down their whole fleet, and some ships fled to the sea.

With their formation broken, the Spanish were blocked off and forced to retreat amid terrible weather conditions. The Spanish Armada was soundly defeated, and England reveled in its victory.

In a few short decades, warfare went from medieval skirmishes to sophisticated naval battles. The Tudor era was marked by significant battles that changed the fortunes of Tudor monarchs and led to serious advancements in their weapons and military. As the

Tudors went from battle to battle, they were forced to rethink the way their army was structured, and this helped them to win some of their most significant battles.

Chapter 10: The Military and the Royal Navy

Medieval warfare was as interesting as it was brutal and barbaric. The medieval times included periods of immense changes and wars that ravaged Europe. During this time, great advancements were made in warfare and military tactics. When the Wars of the Roses began, England was stuck in an internal struggle that saw local nobles fight bitterly against one another. The age of English military glory under strong Plantagenet kings was long gone. As a result of the stagnation caused by the civil war, when the Tudors came to power, the English army used the same types of weapons and military tactics as they had during the Hundred Years' War against France.

However, under the ever-enthusiastic and ambitious Henry VIII, things began to change rapidly, as the king built up a mighty fleet spearheaded by impressive warships. A study of the military and army during the Tudor era provides invaluable insight into the rapidly changing times that the Tudors oversaw and the mindset of a continent that was slowly advancing from the Dark Ages toward the Enlightenment.

Medieval English Military Tactics

There are three specific periods of warfare during medieval England that helped advance the army and its military tactics. These periods were the Norman Conquest, the Hundred Years' War, and the Wars of the Roses. The Norman Conquest introduced castles and mounted armored knights to English warfare. English footmen were woefully outmatched by mounted Norman knights at the Battle of Hastings. While the English fought bravely, they were overrun by the Norman cavalry, which used spears to their advantage. Knights who were seated on horses had impressive capabilities, as they had the higher ground and were firmly anchored on their mounts. From their lofty position, they were able to strike precisely at their enemies.

The first English castles were simple structures protected by wooden blockades. These were built by the Normans. These buildings allowed the army to keep supplies and were easily defensible positions. Soon, wooden blockades were replaced with stone, and English kings recognized the usefulness of castles and began building them and keeps throughout the country. Unfortunately, it soon became apparent that these early rectangular castles were vulnerable to siege warfare, which led to the necessity of different shapes, such as polygonal and cylindrical castles.

37. Totnes Castle, Devon

As England engaged in more wars, its mounted knights received more sophisticated weapons, such as the longbows. These weapons gave England a distinct advantage, which could be seen at the Battle of Agincourt. However, while many nobles used horses to go to war, most of these battles were fought on foot. In time, cannons and firearms were used in warfare, but these early guns were difficult to transport and load, which often proved to be disastrous during battle. Thanks to the efforts of the Norman conquerors and the Plantagenet kings, England was well equipped and ready to go to war with its enemies. However, toward the end of the Plantagenet dynasty, the fighting in England turned inward once the nobility ripped itself apart.

Military Recruitment

In the medieval era, the king could call his nobles to battle, and his nobles had to respond to the summons by raising an army of fighting men from their lands. However, this meant that nobles often had fighting forces at the ready to further their own causes. It also meant that the majority of the king's fighting forces were made up of men who weren't trained for war; rather, they were farmers and other ordinary men. Many nobles responded to this problem by keeping a highly skilled force of knights and household troops.

Sometimes, mercenaries had to be hired to make up numbers or provide a skilled fighting force.

From the time of the Norman Conquest, it became apparent that knights were an invaluable asset in an army, so kings rewarded a knight's loyal service with gifts of land. These gifts came with strings, though; a knight was duty bound to heed a call to arms. For some time, there was a law in England that required every man to fight for forty days, but that wasn't enough time to complete a military campaign. This eventually gave way to the scutage arrangement, where a man could pay to be let out of his military obligation and allowed England to keep a standing army. All of this still wasn't enough, and from the 12th century onward, there was a massive mercenary market in Europe. Kings could pay to have a highly skilled fighting force that didn't require continuous maintenance.

These mercenaries often organized themselves into highly skilled bands, which allowed anyone with enough money to temporarily own a small, top-notch army. Unfortunately, these mercenaries were loyal to the highest paying bidder, and they weren't above robbing and looting any towns they came across. Often, mercenaries were foreign men who terrorized the unfortunate countryside where they were let loose.

Henry VII's Army

Henry VII didn't have access to royal funds when he fought the most crucial battle of his life at Bosworth Field. Instead, he had to rely on money from his allies and a force of foreign mercenaries who were only loyal to money. As he marched through England, he managed to amass a larger army than he arrived with, but he was still outnumbered. It was only thanks to the efforts of more experienced commanders and the last-minute assistance from powerful nobles that allowed him to win his crown. Henry VII was aware of this fact and knew that he had taken possession of a country where nobles were used to raising armies on a whim.

Henry declared himself king by right of conquest, which meant that anyone who fought with Richard III was guilty of treason. Henry VII could also take hold of all of Richard III's properties and resources. He then made all the nobles swear fealty to him under the threat of losing their lands. Due to the constant threat of rebellion, Henry VII had his own personal security force to protect him from any kind of danger and restrict access to the royal family.

In an effort to bring peace to his troubled country, Henry VII appointed many justices of the peace, which were men who served a shire for a year and were then replaced. They were in charge of overseeing law enforcement in their area and were instrumental in bringing justice after the lawlessness of the civil war. However, Henry VII wisely curbed their power. Since the justices of the peace had a lot of influence, minor nobles were eager to join their ranks, which gave Henry VII more control over them.

Unlike other European leaders at the time, Henry VII did little to advance his army, and men were called up as they were needed. Henry VII faced the unenviable task of building up royal funds after the Wars of the Roses, and he didn't have enough money to spare on a permanent army. Besides, a large royal army could fall into the wrong hands, and Henry VII was well aware of the many threats that surrounded his kingship.

The Ban on Private Armies

While Henry VII had to deal with many problems when he became king, the problem of retaining was one that most of his predecessors had also faced. This practice allowed nobles to use lower-born men to advance their interests in the area, which often included taking up arms. Nobles were allowed to give out livery or uniforms and badges to their followers. Another facet of retaining was that of maintenance, as nobles were allowed to keep numerous male servants who could also act as soldiers if necessary.

In the past, kings were forced to accept retaining since nobles felt they needed to keep their lands through force and were responsible for keeping peace on their properties. Kings could also rely on retainers to support their military campaigns, although as time progressed, it became clear that powerful nobles could use their power to influence the outcome of key battles. This was clearly evidenced during the Wars of the Roses. While Henry VII had benefited from strong nobles, he wasn't willing to allow the practice to continue.

As soon as he became king, he made his thoughts about retaining clear when he condemned the practice. While he couldn't directly outlaw it, he went through a lot of effort to restrict it. Nobles were allowed to participate in "lawful retaining," which included keeping a retainer for the purpose of serving the king. If a noble wanted to participate, he had to get a license from the Privy Council that only lasted until the king died. Henry also set laws on livery and maintenance, which restricted the nobles' power.

Henry VII is also accredited with strengthening the English navy. He commissioned the dry dock at Portsmouth, which would become the home of the Royal Navy. While Henry VII had many problems to deal with, in many ways, he set the stage for much of Henry VIII's triumphs.

Henry VIII's Royal Army

When Henry VIII inherited the throne, England's army was slightly behind the times. The soldiers still used outdated weapons, such as cavalry lances and bows. Henry VII wasn't particularly military-minded and preferred to focus on saving money for the royal treasury, but young Henry VIII was determined to advance the English military. He began by encouraging the production of arms and armor on English soil and went out of his way to bring more advanced weapons into the country.

38. Guards during the reign of Henry VIII

His soldiers became familiar with the pike and hand firearms, which had traditionally been reserved for foreign mercenaries. While Henry VIII had high hopes for his army and put a lot of effort into reforming it, he still needed to hire large numbers of foreign mercenaries when he went to France in 1544. Unfortunately for the king, who dreamed of advancing England's military, scholars have paid little attention to Henry VIII's military exploits since his army fought mostly with outdated weapons and tactics. During this same time, the Italian Wars were being fought. These wars helped enhance warfare in Europe and saw great innovations, while Henry VIII's wars were smaller and less influential by comparison.

While the English still used tactics that helped them win the Battle of Agincourt, France's and Burgundy's cavalries used pikes and guns, which gave them the advantage on the field. However, it has been theorized that Henry VIII had probably been wise not to suddenly abandon traditional English fighting methods since Europe was still experimenting with new technology. During that time, firearms were still being developed and were cumbersome, inaccurate weapons that failed against experienced archers. In time, firearms would become deadlier and more accurate, but for the time being, the English probably didn't see the need to reproduce clumsy firearms when their archers were more capable of winning battles.

Gun Forts

Medieval castles helped fend off a variety of enemies, but they were essentially homes with heavy fortifications. The Tudor era saw the rise of gun forts, which were military buildings that were constructed with the sole purpose of assisting in battles. The forts that were built during the Tudor era would stand for centuries and be useful in future wars. Henry VIII saw their potential and built over thirty forts along the English coast between the years 1539 and 1547. It would prove to be the first project of its kind since the Romans. When Henry VIII caused the dramatic split between the Church of England and the Roman Church, he faced the wrath of Catholic powers in Europe, which threatened to invade England with the divine approval of the papacy. As a result, Henry VIII needed to defend his shores, and the gun forts helped him to do that.

39. Pendennis Castle

These gun forts were simple round structures that would withstand fire from enemy ships and provide a place for English gunners to fire on foreign fleets. If an enemy armada tried to invade England, the ships would find themselves under heavy fire as soon as they approached the coast. The forts were fitted with "ship-killing" guns that would deter any potential enemies. Henry VIII built gun forts all along England' Nil fanion, southern and eastern coasts. It was surely one of the highlights of his reign, and the king kept his forts well stocked at all times. The forts proved to be so useful that Elizabeth I used them when she faced the Spanish Armada. Over the years, the structures were renovated with more advanced weapons, and more sophisticated architecture was added. In fact, the gun forts were so effective that some of them were used in the Second World War.

Henry VIII's Royal Navy

Despite the fact that Henry VII didn't show much military ambition, he still began the project of building warships before he died. When Henry VIII took the throne, he had five warships at his disposal. He began building up a formidable Navy so that by the time he died, the navy was made up of more than forty ships. He began building dockyards in 1512 in Deptford and Woolwich, which were located near his own palace at Greenwich, likely so that he could keep a close eye on his pet project. He also built the dockyard at Portsmouth, which would prove useful when facing future threats of invasion.

Almost as soon as Henry VIII began building up the navy, he realized that more was needed than dockyards and ships. Along with his new naval bases, he also had to build massive storehouses, and he began looking for top-notch supplies for his navy. The king also founded the Navy Board, which would deal with the daily duties of caring for the navy. The first warships were made out of wood, but they were powerful vessels that could inflict a lot of damage in battle.

Unlike past ships, Henry VIII's ships had to transport dozens of massive cannons, which were situated all along one side of the ship and could be fired at the same time, causing devastating damage to enemy ships. While these cannons were a game changer, they also presented a unique problem. How could they stick out of the ship without allowing water through the holes they were aimed through? As a result, gunports were invented. Cannons were pointed through these holes during battle, but they were each fitted with watertight flaps on hinges that could be closed while the ship was sailing. This allowed more guns to be fitted to ships, and cannons were taken further down the ship so that the vessel didn't become unbalanced. Henry VIII's warships were massive ships that were fitted with twenty heavy cannons and sixty light cannons. The ships carried hundreds of people into war. While the navy was a source of immense pride to the vain king, his flagship, the *Mary Rose*, was the crown jewel of his naval achievements.

The *Mary Rose*

Before Henry VIII, kings had to hire merchant ships if they needed to go to war. This had the advantage of being cheaper than keeping a navy, but it was a time-consuming practice that could cost valuable time when facing the threat of invasion. Henry VIII knew that it was only a matter of time before an enemy country showed up on English shores with a more advanced fleet. As a result, he began building up his navy with enthusiasm, and he soon had dozens of ships. However, none were as special to him as his flagship, the *Mary Rose*.

40. The *Mary Rose*

The *Mary Rose* may have been built as early as 1510, along with *Peter Pomegranate*, in Portsmouth. While there are claims that the ship was named after Henry VIII's favorite sister, Mary, it's more likely that the ship was named after the Virgin Mary, who was known as the "Mystic Rose" in those times. The ship was fitted with powerful cannons and gun ports, which made it one of the most technically advanced ships of its time. By the time Henry VIII declared war on France in 1512, his flagship was completed and ready to carry the king toward military glory.

The ship was used at the Battle of Saint-Mathieu in 1512 and as a transport ship during the Battle of Flodden in 1513. By 1514, the war in France was winding down, and the ship was decommissioned and left at Portsmouth. However, when Henry VIII went to France in 1520 for the meeting of the Field of the Cloth of Gold, Henry VIII chose to take his favorite ship with him to display his wealth and glory to his old enemy. For the next few years, the *Mary Rose* took part in the skirmishes against France, but it was mostly inactive until 1539, when Henry VIII faced serious threats of invasion from Catholic European powers.

In 1544, Henry VIII went to war against France and won Boulogne, which led to the Battle of the Solent. This battle would have tragic consequences for his beloved flagship. While engaged in the battle, the ship turned suddenly. The wind pressed the ship down, and her starboard side was pushed into the water. Unfortunately, the gunports were all open, and the ship took on massive amounts of water and sank in a little over half an hour. Hundreds of men died while the battle raged on. Henry VIII was forced to watch as his beloved ship disappeared under the waves.

Attempts were made to raise the ship from the depths, but the *Mary Rose* would remain below the water until 1982.

Elizabeth I's Fleet

When Elizabeth I took the throne, piracy was a massive problem, as pirates roamed the seas virtually unchecked. As a result, they plundered merchant ships, which caused heavy losses for England. Elizabeth I countered this problem by commissioning privateers. These men were private merchants who were authorized to attack and loot pirate ships, although they were mostly used to plunder Spanish ships returning with riches from the New World. The Spanish Armada was growing at a rapid rate, and instead of engaging with the fleet directly, Elizabeth I's privateers, or "Sea Dogs," would pick off individual ships and rob them, which helped reduce Spain's wealth and power.

Some of her most notable Sea Dogs were Sir Walter Raleigh and Sir Francis Drake. These men were known as adventurers and for being competent naval officers. Sir Francis Drake helped the queen against the Spanish Armada. While the Spaniards condemned the Sea Dogs, Elizabeth I used her privateers to great advantage along with her official navy.

While the Tudor era was defined by dramatic social changes and climatic religious reforms, it was also a time of advancement for the national military and the foundation of the Royal Navy. As the military advanced, the need arose for new and more sophisticated weapons.

Chapter 11: Tudor Weapons

When the Tudor era began, Europe was in the midst of a time of great change and upheaval. Various wars led to the development of modern weapons and the rejection of medieval military tactics. By the time England emerged from the Wars of the Roses, its military had stagnated, and it was vastly behind its peers. While it managed to successfully wage wars against countries like Ireland and Scotland, it was only able to win the majority of those battles since those countries were on the same footing. While Europe was fighting massive wars, such as the Italian Wars, England's days of large-scale foreign conquests seemed to be over.

However, when Henry VIII was an energetic young man who didn't have the same haunted and wary tendencies as Henry VII, who narrowly won the Battle of Bosworth Field. Henry VIII quickly began reforming his military and investigating the new weapons that were making their debut in Europe. The Tudor era saw a rapid change in England's military, going from conventional weapons to gunpowder weapons. The English army used a mixture of both types of weapons until gunpowder weapons became more sophisticated and prevalent.

Traditional Tudor Weapons

Although the Tudor period was a time of change for the English military, the traditional medieval weapons had seen great success at legendary battles, such as Agincourt. The change from traditional weapons to modern weapons was gradual. English soldiers and weapons manufacturers weren't unaware of modern weapons. After all, they were exposed to foreign mercenaries who brought their weapons with them. However, it's likely that they weren't impressed by what they saw. In the beginning, gunpowder weapons were inconvenient and took time to load, which may have made the traditional bow and pike weapons seem vastly superior in the hands of experienced soldiers.

- Longbow

The English longbow was a popular weapon during medieval times for hunting and warfare. It stood at about six feet tall and is thought to have had a range of about four hundred yards. This would have allowed experienced archers to stay well away from the battlefield and rain deadly arrows upon their enemies with accuracy. The arrows would have used steel points that could easily penetrate mail armor.

Longbows were used during the Hundred Years' War against France, and the Tudors adopted the weapon into their arsenal. This is evidenced by the fact that thousands of arrows and over a hundred longbows were found aboard the *Mary Rose* when it was salvaged.

- Ballock Dagger

The ballock (or bollock) dagger was popular in Europe from the 13th century to the late 18th century. It was a simple weapon with a hilt that had two oval shapes near the guard that was supposed to aid with grip. These oval shapes looked like male testes, thus leading to the distinctive name. The weapon served as a last resort when a soldier's lance and/or sword failed. Most soldiers carried this type of dagger, and hundreds were found aboard the *Mary Rose.*

- Battle-ax

Battle-axes have a long history that predates the Tudor era by several centuries. The earliest battle-axes were little more than normal axes that were used to smash enemies to pieces. In time, battle-axes became more specialized. During the Tudor era, battle-axes were about thirty centimeters (one foot) in length and varied in weight according to what had been added to the weapon. Many horsemen used an ax while charging since it was unwieldy to use in close combat. Battle-axes had sharp pikes attached to the top and back of the blade to give the weapon extra penetrating power.

- Caltrop

A caltrop was an ingenious weapon that consisted of a long pole with a sharp spike at the top. They were traditionally used by knights at a long distance, but caltrops also caused devastating damage to cavalrymen when they were planted with their spikes facing up. The horses would charge into the field of caltrops and get seriously injured. These types of tactics proved to be fatal on the battlefield, but the caltrops needed to be supplemented by other weapons. A soldier couldn't rely on caltrops alone.

42. Caltrops

- Billhooks

A bill or billhook was a tool that could be used to trim trees or inflict damage on enemy soldiers. They were especially popular during the times when a noble called on his men to march into war since they could be used by soldiers or farmers. Billhooks could be adapted for whatever purpose they needed to accomplish. Some variations had spikes or sharp points that accompanied the hooks. They were often used in conjunction with longbows and were notably used at the Battle of Flodden. Billhooks were used through most of the Tudor era and were a traditional medieval weapon that survived the test of time due to their simplicity and usefulness.

43. Medieval Billhook

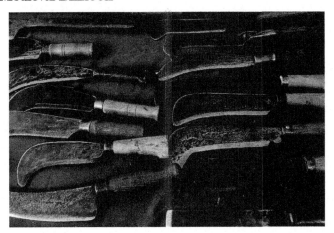

- Lances

Lances were popularly used by knights in jousts, but they could also be used in battle. They were long weapons with a sharp point that could be used to charge at an enemy. During a joust, two knights would charge at each other on horseback, aiming to break the other's lance or pierce the other knight's armor. While the knights weren't trying to hurt each other, these jousts were extremely dangerous. Henry VII nearly died on two separate occasions while jousting. Medieval knights were known to carry lances into war with them, but they could prove to be cumbersome if used incorrectly.

- Halberd

Halberds were pole weapons that were essentially ax blades with a sharp spike on top of a long pole. They were popular from medieval times to well into the Tudor era. In the hands of experienced halberdiers, they were devastating weapons that could be used at long range to kill enemy soldiers. It's possible that either a halberd or a billhook was used to kill Richard III at the Battle of Bosworth. Halberds were effective when used to attack other pikemen, but they were ineffective in the hands of foot soldiers when it came to a cavalry charge or gunpowder weapons.

- Spears

Spears were used by some of the earliest warriors, but they weren't used much during the Tudor era. They were rarely taken to war since they were more useful for close combat. By the Tudor era, battles were increasingly being fought with longer-range weapons. Spears are simple weapons, and there were much more sophisticated weapons that were widely available to common soldiers. That doesn't mean that no one used spears, as there is some evidence that at least some soldiers still preferred them.

Gunpowder Weapons

As the Tudor era progressed, gunpowder weapons became increasingly popular. While they were cumbersome and inconvenient at first, their potential was explosive. As they became more common, they slowly replaced the English longbow, which had long been a favorite for English soldiers. The use of gunpowder led to other innovations, as it became necessary to protect gunpowder from the elements. Cannons were fitted to warships, and gun forts were used to protect England from Catholic invasions. The Tudor forces also found that gunpowder weapons were useful in siege warfare, and slowly, the English army fully embraced these sophisticated weapons.

- Muskets

Muskets arrived in Europe in the 1520s, and the immediate response was armor becoming thicker. Unfortunately, thicker armor was very heavy and expensive. As armor became thicker, larger guns that released more powerful bullets were used, making armor ineffective. Muskets were heavy, but they could be used during sieges or to fight off invaders from a longer distance. As muskets became more sophisticated and powerful, they outmatched longbows. Tudor era soldiers were forced to keep up with the times or face armies with guns while only wielding arrows and bows. Eventually, the choice was clear.

- Cannons

For most of medieval history, castles were effectively forts that could withstand sieges and remain standing while wars and battles raged around them. However, the onset of cannons saw the popularity of castles decline, as cannons could destroy castle walls and make sieges much shorter. Enemy forces could fire continuously at castle walls, and within a few weeks or even days, the castle would be overrun by enemy forces. Henry VIII appreciated the potential of cannons and used them at Boulogne, in his navy, and in his gun forts. Cannons varied according to their purpose and could be larger or smaller as was needed. They were essentially large guns that shot massive cannonballs and became an important part of Tudor warfare.

44. Tudor era cannon

- Arquebus

The arquebus was an early form of the gunpowder weapons that are prevalent in modern times. It first appeared in the Ottoman Empire and in Europe in the 1500s. It was essentially a handgun with a hook-like mechanism that allowed it to be attached to walls or armaments. The advent of the matchlock mechanism allowed muskets to become smaller and more like handguns. As the use of the arquebus became more widespread, armies began to support arquebusiers, who were infantrymen armed with the weapon. The large arquebus became known as the musket, which eventually became the term that was used to refer to all long guns.

45. Soldier with an arquebus

• Matchlock Mechanism

The matchlock mechanism allowed arquebusiers to use shorter weapons that were easier to wield in battle. It also allowed the gunpowder weapons to be equipped with a trigger that made it easier to fire. A matchlock mechanism was essentially a device that ignited gunpowder by burning a small piece of rope when an arquebusier pulled the trigger. Unfortunately, they were difficult to load, which slowed their popularity. It seems that the matchlock firearms originated in the Ottoman Empire before being transported to Europe.

- Flintlock Mechanism

Before triggers, people had to use one arm to steady the arquebus and the other to light the gunpowder, which was a difficult and inconvenient process. However, the matchlock mechanism changed the way guns were used since it introduced the trigger. In time, the matchlock was replaced by the flintlock. The matchlock was inconvenient, as it required the shooter to light a match to ignite the mechanism. The flintlock used flint to ignite the gunpowder and was much easier to use. Unfortunately, it was only developed in the 17th century.

Swords

Many different swords were used during the Tudor era. Swords had been used during many periods in history and were still immensely popular during Tudor times. There were many different types of swords, and they were used for different occasions. Swords could be personalized, which meant that they could be passed on through the generations. During the Tudor period, there were three types of swords that were especially popular. Many experienced soldiers who could afford swords chose to use the weapon, even though gunpowder weapons were becoming increasingly popular. Although other weapons became outdated during the Tudor era, the use of swords remained widespread throughout the period.

- Cutting Sword

By the time the Tudor era began, the cutting sword was already declining in popularity. Throughout most of the medieval period, cutting swords proved to be useful on the battlefield. Swords are ancient weapons that went through many changes over the years. Norman conquerors began to develop cross-guards in the 11th century, which helped to stabilize the weapon. As the Tudor era progressed, armor became more advanced and sophisticated, which made it more difficult for swords to inflict wounds. The swords had to be modified to cut specifically at weaknesses in the armor. The cutting swords of the past had to be exchanged for sleeker, thinner weapons.

- Broadsword

In medieval times, people had different swords for different occasions. Traditionally, broadswords had basket hilts that protected a warrior's hand. They were heavy instruments that were better for cutting at enemies. A broadsword was a lethal weapon that could take down many enemies depending on the soldier's strength and skill level. However, it was too heavy to use for duels, fencing, or ceremonies. A broadsword usually had a longer hilt so that it could be used with both hands.

- Rapier

Fencing was a popular sport among noblemen in the Tudor era, and the advent of the rapier made the sport much more enjoyable. Unlike the heavy cutting swords used by the military, rapiers were sleek and light, which made them perfect for thrusting and lunging at enemies. Rapiers became so popular that noblemen took their rapiers wherever they went, and they became an accessory to complement any nobleman's wardrobe. The rapier originated in continental Europe and allowed a person to move quickly and strike at a distance.

46. Different rapiers

Tudor Soldiers

As the army evolved in the Tudor era, it became necessary to change the way that the army was structured. This restructuring happened gradually, as ordinary soldiers changed their traditional weapons for more sophisticated instruments of war. While some traditional posts were kept, many conventional institutions changed. Henry VII saw the need to employ a permanent force of guards, and when Henry VIII took the throne, he found a way to renew the nobility's interest in the military. By the time the Elizabethan era began, a lot of things had changed in the army from Henry VII's day.

- The Yeomen of the Guard

The Yeomen of the Guard was founded by Henry VII in 1485. These men traditionally wear the Tudor costume. Although the Tower of London had Yeomen Warders, the two companies weren't related. The Yeomen of the Guard was tasked with protecting the monarch in all aspects of his life. They traveled with the monarch and even tasted their food to make sure it hadn't been poisoned. Many former English monarchs hadn't felt the need to create such a force, but Henry VII had every right to be wary after spending most of his life fighting off potential usurpers. Due to the guards' duties, they were the only standing military force in the country.

- The Gentlemen Pensioners

Henry VIII saw a way to involve the nobility in his own protection by creating the Troop of Gentlemen, which was made up of the sons of noble families. This gave the younger sons of noble families who didn't stand to inherit a way to interact with the monarchy and a chance to rise above their stations. The Troop was a mounted force armed with spears and lances. The men rode with the king and ensured his safety. By protecting the king, they also enhanced their own prestige and impressed their importance on everyone around them.

- Infantry

As the army was revitalized, so were the weapons of infantrymen. Henry VIII's infantry force was made up of pikemen, billmen, and archers. In time, archers were replaced with capable gunmen. While Henry VIII admired and imported the newer weapons, most of his forces still carried traditional weapons when he went to war in 1544. It wasn't until the Elizabethan period that gunpowder weapons began to outnumber conventional weapons. Infantry forces were usually divided into smaller companies that were comprised of pikemen in the middle and archers on the flanks.

- Cavalry

In the past, knights had been one of the most important components of any army, but as soldiers were being trained with more sophisticated weapons, it became apparent that the days of knights were numbered. For one thing, their armor wasn't strong enough to withstand the increasing power of gunpowder weapons, and the use of lances and swords failed when faced with weapons that could be shot from a distance. However, the cavalry was a valuable part of the Tudor army. It was usually made up of mounted nobles who paid for their own armor and weapons. As older weapons became obsolete, the mounted forces would use pistols when they went to war.

Foreign Mercenaries

Henry VIII had great dreams for his army, but like his contemporaries and predecessors, he was forced to rely on foreign mercenaries to boost his numbers when he went to war. Mercenaries were highly skilled soldiers who sometimes formed large bands that could be hired for a military campaign. Since it was very expensive to keep a standing army made up of skilled warriors, mercenaries seemed like a necessary evil. Since foreign mercenaries fought alongside English soldiers, the English had a chance to learn about the weapons and tactics that were being used in Europe.

- Landsknechte

The Landsknechte were German pikemen. They were some of the most effective soldiers of their time. They were highly trained individuals who spent most of their time fighting for the highest bidder. These mercenaries used pikes and halberds with ease and were used to moving quickly. Their shock tactics caught their enemies off-guard, and they could even hold their own against a cavalry charge. It is no wonder that Henry VIII used them in his army. They were brutal warriors who fought without mercy and were among the most feared mercenaries in Europe. At first, Henry VIII had access to the Landsknechte since they were created by Maximilian I, the Holy Roman emperor, who loaned several companies to Henry VIII during his war with France. After all, Catherine of Aragon was related to the emperor.

- Stradioti

The Stradioti were mercenaries hired from the Balkans who used Byzantine and Balkan war tactics. They were experienced cavalrymen, which made them attractive to many military leaders since cavalrymen were always in short supply. The Stradioti were able to pioneer many cavalry tactics, which put them ahead of their competition and made them deadly on the battlefield. They were highly skilled men who used complicated tactics that caught their enemies by surprise and were especially adept at traps and ambushes.

- Spanish and Italian Arquebusiers

As gunpowder weapons became more popular in Europe, soldiers who fought in the Italian Wars and other conflicts in Europe had a lot of experience with the new weapons. Once those wars ended, highly skilled soldiers became mercenaries who offered their expertise to anyone who would have them. Henry VIII used these men when he went to war against France, especially in 1544, as his own men had to be trained to use the new weapons since they were mostly archers and pikemen. In time, the English army had its own skilled arquebusiers, leaving behind their traditional bows.

The Tudor era was marked by periods of climatic change, and their army reflected those changes. As newer, more sophisticated weapons were invented, the Tudor forces used a mix of conventional and new weapons to their advantage and held their own against Europe.

Part Four: Life in Tudor England

Chapter 12: Politics and Economy

The Tudor era was a remarkable time that featured some of the most influential monarchs in English history. These rulers lived lavishly and spent extraordinary amounts of money on their projects. This leads to a question; where did they get all that money? The answer lies in England's economy. The rulers had to be careful to stimulate the economy so they could keep up their lifestyles. However, when the economy declined, not only did they have to curb their spending habits, but they also faced serious riots and rebellions that threatened their way of life.

Furthermore, the Tudor court was a dangerous place filled with manipulative schemers who would do anything to get ahead and make a name for themselves. Many individuals within the Tudor government managed to take advantage of the social, political, and religious changes that took place. As Henry VIII proved, the fortunes of entire lineages rested on the whims of a monarch. In an effort to solve his "Great Matter," Henry VIII was willing to forever change the Church of England and put his people through incredible religious reforms. This change had far-reaching consequences that impacted both politics and the economy. In time, England left the medieval era and entered the Renaissance. Elizabeth I found new and creative ways to stimulate the economy, as well as a unique approach to politics.

Agriculture

In Tudor England, many farmers didn't own the land that they worked; instead, they rented land from rich landowners who were usually part of the nobility. Sometimes, the land the farmers rented didn't produce enough to feed them and their families, which meant they had to spend some of their time working as laborers on larger farms. If a person couldn't afford to rent a piece of land, they would work exclusively as laborers. However, most villages had common lands that provided small game for hunting. Farmers who owned animals could let their animals graze on that land.

Agriculture formed a large part of England's economy, and farmers helped landowners become rich, which, in turn, enriched the monarchy. When there were good harvests, there was more than enough to sell and eat, which benefited everyone. However, when the harvests failed, people relied on common lands or handouts from the rich. If a harvest failed, a monarch would have to arrange relief efforts and find ways to stimulate the economy.

Common lands were an important part of a peasant's lifestyle, as they often depended on hunting rabbits for food when times were tough. However, when the cloth trade began to increase, sheep became a valuable commodity due to their wool, and more land was needed for the animals to graze. Large landowners realized they could profit more from raising sheep than renting out their land, so they began charging exorbitant rents. This forced their tenants to abandon the land that they previously farmed. In many communities, rich landowners began closing off large pieces of common land for their sheep. This caused serious problems since peasants weren't allowed to use the land that had sustained them for centuries. As a result, there was a massive outcry, and many peasants revolted. In 1549, there was a huge rebellion led by Robert

Kett, who encouraged peasants to destroy fences that closed off common land.

These rebellions were often defeated since peasants had little to no military expertise and very few weapons. In the case of the Kett rebellion, Edward VI's government sent a force made up of mostly foreign mercenaries who outmatched the peasant army in every way. They brutally put down the rebellion. In time, Parliament tried to fix the matter by imposing laws against enclosures, but since landowners were often in charge of enforcing those laws, they would simply keep the enclosures where they were.

English Wool Trade

The most important commodity that England produced during the Tudor era was wool. English wool was widely considered to be vastly superior to other types of wool. It was often exported in its raw form to Europe, where it was turned into woolen cloth and sold for a massive profit, which benefited England greatly.

The Tudor monarchy, especially under Henry VII, found ways to profit off the wool trade by placing taxes on wool exports, which earned a lot of money. In time, English farmers began to include sheep rearing in their other work. However, the wool industry was seasonally based, which meant that farmers often had other projects too. At first, individuals owned flocks of sheep, but as the Tudor era progressed, rich landowners began amassing larger flocks. Many individuals couldn't afford to keep sheep anymore. The government tried to limit the number of sheep that one person could own, but once again, these laws were largely ignored.

Sheep rearing was a lot of work and provided jobs for peasants. Merchants would fund a lot of the wool trade process, which included shearing sheep, dyeing, and cleaning. The wool trade made up the largest part of England's foreign trade market, and places such as Calais were valuable ports in the trading system. It's estimated that the wool trade made up 90 percent of England's overseas trade during Henry VII's reign.

However, rearing sheep could be difficult, and the wool trade could be impacted by a number of different factors. Europe was prone to outbreaks of war, which could put a complete halt on the wool trade. Even if England didn't participate in the war, its economy was still affected. Another factor was the plague. The plague spread quickly through merchant ships, which meant that if there was an outbreak, trade ground to a halt.

Sheep are also delicate creatures that don't deal well with too much rain. They could also pick up diseases or parasites that would affect their wool production. The wool trade was incredibly profitable, but it could be extremely delicate, which made it risky to base the country's economy on it. Besides wool, England also exported lead, tin, and coal.

The Privy Council

During the Tudor era, the Privy Council was one of the most important parts of the government. The council was involved in the administration of the country, policymaking, and justice. It was also the source of a lot of the political conflicts that affected the Tudor period. It was essential to the Tudor monarchs and was usually made up of experienced men, trusted allies, or the monarch's favorites. Unlike the privy councils in other European countries, the Tudors' Privy Council had a lot of authority, and sometimes, they didn't need the monarch to sign off on their decisions.

The duties of a monarch were numerous and seriously impacted the country, which meant that they needed councilors who could give advice and help make good decisions. The nobility was made up of the monarchs' peers and often provided a useful pool from which to choose advisors and favorites. During medieval times, monarchs made up their own councils or chose their own advisors. While Parliament was a formal institution that met at times, the monarch's advisors met whenever they required assistance. While the advisors handled serious matters, they were somewhat less formal than the proceedings that took place in Parliament.

Henry VII had hundreds of councilors who were charged with a variety of different duties, but he didn't have a privy council and chose to be involved in the intimate details of ruling his country. However, everything changed with Henry VIII. When he took the throne, he relied on a small number of his father's trusted advisors. In 1515, Thomas Wolsey became the Lord Chancellor and began organizing the council more effectively. For the next few years, Henry VIII was advised by an "inner ring" of councilors. Wolsey fell out of favor when he failed to resolve the king's "Great Matter." In 1530, Thomas Cromwell joined the inner ring, and the king's annulment soon became a reality.

It was only around 1536 that the "inner ring" was identified as the Privy Council. The Privy Council was incredibly important, and Henry VIII chose his son's council before he died. When Mary and Elizabeth took the throne, they each chose their own councilors.

Local Government

England was divided into counties or shires, which made it easier to dispense justice and handle administrative affairs. The most important offices of local government were those of the sheriff and the Lord Lieutenant. The sheriff was appointed to a term of one year, and all appointments were made through the Privy Council. He would be responsible for choosing under-sheriffs and bailiffs who would assist him in dispensing justice. His duties included presiding over a monthly court that took care of any criminal cases, enforcing judgments, and running the jail.

The office of Lord Lieutenant was created by Henry VIII. The men appointed to this office were responsible for representing the king in each county. They were tasked with dealing with the local nobility and arranging the local military. This impressed the king's authority throughout the country and took care of the intricacies of mobilizing a local military force when the king called them to arms. A Lord Lieutenant also had the important task of trying to keep the local gentry happy when the army mobilized, as there was a culture of petty infighting when the king called his men to arms, as everyone wanted the honor of leading the force. The Lord Lieutenant had an enviable measure of power, and it was a potentially risky office for the king, but Henry VIII made sure to curb their power and set up a chain of command that prevented any ambitious rebellions.

While military and judicial matters were taken care of by sheriffs and Lord Lieutenants, there were also justices of the peace. These men were responsible for administrative tasks. Constables, mayors, aldermen, and churchwardens were other facets of the local government during the Tudor era. Unfortunately, many of these positions were filled by the nobility, who chose their friends or favorites to occupy other important roles within the local government. This system didn't offer much representation for peasants or the lower classes, which meant that their complaints often went unheard. In many cases, laws were ignored if they didn't benefit the nobility, such as the laws about enclosures and the size of sheep herds. During times of trouble, peasants often felt they had no other option but to rebel since it was clear that the justice system had failed them.

The Reformation Parliament

When King Henry VIII broke away from the Catholic Church, the split had serious political consequences. In the past, the church had been under the jurisdiction of the papacy, but in solving the "Great Matter," Henry VIII allowed Parliament to be involved in religious matters. This meant that the government had authority over every aspect of national life. It also allowed Henry VIII to change religious doctrine and institute the religious reform that would allow him to get divorced from Catherine of Aragon. Parliament was extremely busy during this time, as it had to pass laws that stripped the pope's authority in England.

Soon, the church was stripped of many of its privileges. The clergy were allowed to be tried like any other subjects in England

and wouldn't be given preferential treatment in the eyes of the law. Parliament passed a law that prevented people from involving foreign powers in matters of English justice, which effectively allowed Henry VIII to persecute any Catholics who asked the pope for help. Soon, Parliament stepped up its tactics and threatened to deprive the pope of taxes and levies from Catholics in England. This was a massive chunk of income and was usually paid in return for papal authorization of bishop nominations and other church taxes.

Moreover, Parliament was used to pass the Act of Succession and the Act of Supremacy, which made Henry VIII the head of the Church of England and allowed him to divorce Catherine of Aragon. Thomas Cromwell was responsible for many of the acts, and Parliament was mainly responsible for dealing with religious legislation. The "Great Matter" had to be solved at all costs, but the split from Rome meant that there were many administrative matters that had to be put in place before it was possible. After the split from Rome, Henry VIII and his successors used Parliament to pass other laws and statutes during their reigns. Laws were usually more effective when Parliament agreed to enforce them. However, the monarchy and Parliament had to work together closely to keep up this arrangement.

The Economic Consequences of the Reformation

The Catholic Church exerted an enormous amount of influence over Europe during the medieval ages, and during that time, it became incredibly rich. However, as the Protestant Reformation began to spread through the continent, the Catholic Church often reacted violently, which led to many religious conflicts. Despite its efforts, Protestants made a lot of progress, and England eventually split from the church in Rome and began adopting Protestant ideals. In time, the English monarchy and nobility took many resources from the church and put money into their own pockets.

This increased the wealth of many people, and it may have helped to popularize the English Reformation.

For decades, the Catholic Church held the monopoly on religious offices and enriched itself by holding the keys to heaven and imposing spiritual laws on ordinary people. Catholic universities focused on theology, and many graduates became members of the clergy. Protestantism removed much of the mystery surrounding religion, and many people chose to enter secular positions once they left university since the clergy had declined in prominence. This led to economic secularization, which is a theory that suggests prosperity lessens the need for religion and leads to the eventual decline of religion's role in a country.

While England became richer from plundering the church's wealth, the split from Rome also led to some trading restrictions. Catholic countries tried to please the pope by limiting contact with England. This didn't change Henry VIII's mind, though. As the church declined, there wasn't much of a need to build religious buildings in Protestant areas, and people were increasingly employed by secular authorities.

In the past, people used their money to fund the church by paying for levies, taxes, nominations, and indulgences. However, as the national religion changed and such things were condemned, people felt comfortable using their money to stimulate the national economy instead. There were some economic repercussions in terms of trade, but these didn't last long. However, the Reformation led to religious conflict and the threat of invasion, which forced Henry VIII to spend more money on national defense. While there were several unfortunate consequences, the English Reformation also caused a shift in the people's thinking, which eventually benefited the economy. It also served to increase Henry VIII's treasury and enrich several noble families, which made them reluctant to return to Catholicism.

Exploration

As Europe left the medieval era, several European countries began to build ships to explore the seas. Spain became immensely rich after its conquest of the New World. The Spanish brought shiploads of gold back to the continent, which motivated other European countries to begin their own exploratory efforts. Elizabeth I was quick to follow Spain's example. Thanks to her father's efforts, she had a whole fleet of ships at her disposal. She began looking for ways to increase her country's wealth and sent explorers to Asia, the Americas, and Africa, where they would find resources that could be used to enrich England.

These explorers were sometimes referred to as Elizabeth I's Sea Dogs, and they were a major threat to the Spanish. As the Spanish ferried gold between the Americas and Europe, they were sometimes attacked by pirates who would sink their ships and steal their gold. Somehow, that gold managed to make its way back to England, and the queen profited greatly. Tudor explorers took to the seas to look for new trading routes, while some carried religious refugees who were looking for a new land where they could practice their religion in peace. In time, these explorers managed to colonize pieces of territory for England, which served to boost England's economy in incredible ways.

The Tudor period marked a shift from the medieval era to the sophisticated Renaissance era, which had a definite impact on politics and the economy. It also affected English society and education.

Chapter 13: Society and Education in Tudor England

It would be easy to focus on the fascinating lives of the Tudor monarchs and forget about the people they were supposed to take care of, but that would be a mistake. Many interesting factors of Tudor life can be gleaned from taking a look at Tudor society. Since the Tudor era was marked by distinctive times of change, it is worth looking at what society and education were like during these times, as the people who lived through the period had to deal with the trials of living as well as political, economic, and religious changes.

This chapter will delve into the four social classes that made up Tudor society and explain how the different classes lived. It will start at the very top with the nobility who lived in luxury and go down to the bottom classes, which could be executed for refusing an honest day's work. There will also be a quick glance into what education was like in England.

The Nobility

The highest social class in Tudor times was the nobility. The nobles won the "birth lottery," as they were the most powerful class besides the royal family. Some of the most important families and individuals in the Tudor era were from the nobility, and they wielded incredible influence in Tudor society. These were the people who were the closest to the monarchs and, as a result, were able to benefit from a royal's favor. However, if they angered the monarch, they could just as easily lose everything. The nobility was an extremely closed-off class since they didn't want to share their power. The more people who rose up, the less power there was to go around. The people in the nobility were either born into powerful families or were appointed to their positions.

- Food

The nobility had a large and varied diet since they had more access to expensive food. They also usually dined with the king or other nobles, which meant that rich feasts and banquets were typical. At royal banquets, exotic dishes such as conger eel and porpoise were served, along with sweet dishes. Typical banquets had game, meat pies, lambs, swans, and venison. The nobles also had access to the finest wines and beverages, and these dinner parties were usually lively affairs accompanied by entertainment.

- Clothing

Nobles wore flamboyant and high-quality clothes. They often had massive wardrobes filled with expensive clothing. Women wore linen shifts that were changed daily but had intricate outer layers and headdresses. Fashion changed frequently, and the queen or king's mistresses usually influenced courtly fashion.

Headdresses were often heavy and elaborate, and they required women to wear linen caps or hoods underneath. Men wore silk shirts with frills at the wrists and neck. They also wore doublets, which were richly embroidered jackets with striped pants. While men didn't wear headdresses, they often wore ruffs that were starched and pleated garments that fit around their necks.

- Professions

The nobility often didn't have to work. They owned a lot of land and collected rents from their tenants. However, male members of the nobility who were close to the monarch often had high positions within the government. They received favors and responsibilities from the monarch and had a chance to rise higher within the government.

Tudor Sumptuary Laws

Prestige was an important part of being a monarch. Henry VIII put a lot of effort into asserting his glory and prosperity through his portraits, attire, and entertainment. When he entertained foreign ministers, he always made sure to put on a good show so his guests would take reports of his strength and glory back to their own monarchs. He also viewed sumptuary laws as important and revised the Acts of Apparel multiple times during his reign. The nobility was an extension of his own authority, and he wanted to keep the newly rich or common-born people from imitating his court or family.

The sumptuary laws restricted the clothes that people wore so that a strict social hierarchy could be maintained. For example, anyone outside of the family was forbidden to wear the color purple. By restricting the types of clothes that people wore, Henry VIII could impress his own authority and maintain the strict boundaries between social classes. The sumptuary laws had the added benefit of encouraging people to support local textile markets.

During Elizabeth I's era, the sumptuary laws were loosened once the import market grew.

47. Robert Dudley in Garter robes

Besides clothing, the sumptuary laws also limited the amount of money that people could spend on their food and furniture. In Tudor England, status was everything, and a person's clothes told everyone which social class they belonged to. The rich were allowed to wear silk and certain colors, but only the royal family was allowed to wear what they wanted. Royal clothing, particularly ceremonial robes, was trimmed with ermine to represent the royals' advanced status. Below the royalty was the nobility, who were allowed to wear different clothes based on their titles. Those who were above viscounts and barons could wear gold, silver, tinseled satin, cloth with silver or gold, or silk. The viscounts, barons, members of the Privy Council, and the Knights of the Garter were allowed to wear furs, velvet, crimson, gold, silver, or pearls.

The Gentry

The next social class was the gentry. This social class was made up of rich landowners, knights, squires, and gentlemen. If a person didn't have to work with their hands, they were part of the gentry. The gentry exploded during the Elizabethan era and became the most important class of the time. Usually, a person became part of the gentry when they became a knight. From there, they could use their position to build up their fortunes, and in time, they could receive a title that would make them part of the nobility. One could also enter the gentry through marriage, although the gentry often didn't marry below their class.

- Food

Depending on their status, the gentry didn't often eat at court but still had luxurious diets. They would often have swans, peafowl, geese, boars, or deer, as these animals often lived on the lands they owned. Hunting was seen as a gentleman's sport and was a favorite pastime among the rich. They also used herbs, such as rosemary, thyme, sage, and mint, to season their food. The rich also ate manchet, which was a soft bread made out of expensive white flour.

- Clothing

Like the nobility, the gentry spent a lot of time and money on their clothes. Depending on their wealth, women could wear fine floor-length gowns, and men could wear silk shirts and doublets over their trousers. The sumptuary laws were very strict for the gentry, and those who earned over £100 a year were allowed to wear damask, silk, camlet, satin, or taffeta. After that, the sumptuary laws became stricter according to a person's title.

48. Mayor, alderman, and liveryman, 1574

Since many people weren't part of the nobility, they had to pay careful attention to the sumptuary laws, or else they would be fined or face serious repercussions.

• Professions

Like the nobility, many members of the gentry didn't have to work. They owned land and/or businesses or occupied positions within the local government. The gentry often became justices of the peace, Lord Lieutenants, or sheriffs. They were mostly preoccupied with running their estates and taking care of their investments. However, the gentry often had to heed the monarch's call to arms and lead men into battle at their ruler's command. They were often well equipped for battle and had some measure of military training. As the merchant class rose in England, some of them were able to buy their way into the gentry and eventually into the nobility.

The Yeomanry

The "middle class" in Tudor England was known as the yeomanry. They had better jobs than the poor and usually became apprentices when they were young. As a result, they could usually afford to save some money or look for ways to improve their lives. The life of a yeoman consisted of hard work, but their lives were generally better than the poor. However, the people in this class could lose their status very easily in times of plague, famine, or war. Many of the people in this class were servants, tradesmen, or merchants.

- Food

Depending on their profession, the middle class was usually able to get their hands on vegetables, such as cabbages and onions. Eventually, tomatoes, peppers, and potatoes were imported from the New World, but those vegetables were expensive at first. The yeomen usually ate whatever meat they could afford, which was commonly rabbits, hens, pheasants, partridges, ducks, fish, and pigeons. They also ate yeoman's bread or ravel, which was made out of wholemeal.

- Clothing

Under the sumptuary laws, ordinary people couldn't wear silk, jewels, or gold. This was unfortunate for those of the yeoman class, like merchants, who could afford to wear such items. Instead, women usually wore kirtles, which were ankle-length dresses made from wool that had square necks. Wealthier women usually wore a gown over their kirtles. All women had to cover their heads, and they wore linen caps under bonnets or veils. They usually had girdles that were attached to their waist and helped them carry their possessions.

Men usually wore simple leather doublets over their pants and hung their purses or daggers from their belts.

- Professions

Yeomen usually started out as apprentices at the age of fourteen and would work with experienced tradesmen for about seven years until they were able to strike out on their own. During that time, they would live with their master and weren't allowed to get married until they were done with their apprenticeship. Typical professions were cordwainers, weavers, tailors, smiths, masons, and barbers. The yeomanry was also made up of farmers, servants, and merchants. This class usually rose above their station if they made enough money, but this required a lot of money and effort.

The Poor

Unfortunately, this was the largest class during the Tudor era. Many people lost their possessions due to war, illness, or famine. Weather during the Tudor period could be unpredictable, which could lead to bad harvests. This could have disastrous consequences on the whole economy. Furthermore, as enclosures became more common, people who used to have profitable farms suddenly found themselves without a job or home and were forced into a life of extreme poverty. There were some efforts to help the poor (although the poor laws were often meant to punish beggars), but these didn't do much to alleviate the suffering of the lowest class.

- Food

All classes had bread with their meals in Tudor England since it was easy to make, but the quality varied between the classes. The poor usually ate Carter's bread, which was very cheap but made from low-quality ingredients. This bread was made from rye and wheat and was usually quite tough to eat. Ale was a popular beverage since the water was usually dirty or polluted and could cause illnesses. The poor had to rely on whatever meat they could catch, and they often caught rabbits, birds, or fish on common land.

- Clothing

Sumptuary laws didn't really apply to the lower classes since they usually couldn't afford the restricted items. Women wore simple kirtles and linen dresses made from cheap fabric or wool. The poor wore clothing that wasn't very different from the clothing yeomen wore, but they were usually made from cheaper material. The poorer class had fewer clothes as well. Nightgowns were only worn by rich people, and the lower classes simply wore their shifts or smocks when they went to bed.

Poor Laws

For much of English history, monasteries were responsible for supplying aid to the poor and needy. However, once the monasteries closed down, a new system of relief was needed, which led to the poor laws. At first, these laws didn't help the poor and were unforgiving. Anyone who was termed a beggar or vagrant had to be placed in the stocks for a few days before being sent out of town. Later, justices of the peace were allowed to assign begging areas, and anyone who was caught begging would be whipped for laziness instead of being put in the stocks. Eventually, the situation became so dire that collections were taken for the poor in churches.

During Edward VI's reign, the poor laws became harsher. Anyone who was named a vagrant would be branded as a first warning and executed on their second offense. Along with this brutal law, the king also created the position of Collector of Alms in each parish, which would serve to help the poor. Houses of correction were also established to help the poor; these were places of refuge that provided work for the needy.

Mary I also enacted brutal laws, calling for punishments, such as burning through the ear or hanging, for anyone who was a professional beggar. When Elizabeth I took the throne, she ordered everyone who earned money to donate money to the poor and had towns collect resources to help their poor populations.

Tudor Education

Education was an important part of the Tudor era, but there was no state system of schooling. Education was mostly reserved for the rich and powerful. Most of the yeomanry sent their boys into apprenticeships at young ages so that they could learn a trade and look after themselves as they grew older. This meant that a large portion of the population were skilled laborers. Girls weren't usually educated, but they were taught to run households and look after their families. However, the rich classes required their women to run estates, and they sometimes had serious responsibilities that required education. These girls were educated at home by private tutors. Henry VIII's daughters received a top-notch education, which was somewhat unusual at the time.

Rich boys went to leading schools such as St. Anthony's and St. Paul's, where they were taught Latin, mathematics, literature, and geography. In time, schools were opened for orphaned boys and girls. They were funded by rich merchants and taught basic subjects such as writing, reading, and arithmetic. Children usually went to school from early in the morning until the early evening and worked six days a week. They used hornbooks and wrote with feather quills that often had to be sharpened with knives. Discipline was an important part of Tudor education, and students were punished with beatings.

After they left grammar school, some rich boys attended universities, while others were included in the family estate or found some other profession.

Society and education played an important role in the Tudor era, but perhaps one of the most fascinating subjects of the era was that of the church and religion. The Tudor monarchs changed the course of history according to their faiths and beliefs, which meant that England's religion went through incredible changes in just a few short years.

Chapter 14: Religion and the Church

Religion played a major part in daily life in medieval England. Churches were a stable source of comfort and relief, places where people could turn to in times of need. The people's traditions and beliefs gave them hope during difficult times and helped to keep order in the realm. The poor could turn to monasteries when everyone else refused to help them. However, the church also took a lot of money from its people and endorsed various conflicts. While it did help the poor, much of the clergy lived in relative luxury, and a lot of the church's money was sent to the pope in distant Rome.

When the Tudors took the throne, the old religion was dutifully observed by Henry VII and his family, but his focus was on stabilizing the country. In contrast, Henry VIII was a religious man who was well versed in theology. He became obsessed with the notion that his first marriage was cursed and took matters into his own hands. At first, the English Reformation began as a way to solve Henry VIII's "Great Matter," but it led to England becoming a Protestant nation. The sequence of events that led to that monumental shift is fascinating and worth studying.

Religion during Henry VII's Reign

England was a Catholic country when Henry VII was king. His mother, Margaret Beaufort, was an extremely pious woman who had great influence in the early Tudor court. She wouldn't have allowed any hint of religious reforms while she was alive. There were small groups who questioned the Roman Catholic Church, but they were persecuted relentlessly and branded as heretics, a charge that carried some of the heaviest penalties at the time. The royal court faithfully observed the old religious practices, including religious plays, saints' days, and pilgrimages.

Henry VII wasn't particularly interested in religion and focused on other matters during his reign. He had inherited a volatile country and spent much of his reign chasing down pretenders and protecting his family from treason. Margaret Beaufort, by contrast, was fanatically devoted to her religion. She was a powerful patron of the church, regularly gave to the poor, and supported religious studies. Later in life, she made a public vow of chastity and enrolled as a "sister" in several monastic houses. Although she was still married when she took her vow, she was allowed to move away from her husband and live in her own home to fulfill her vow. Margaret's piety was well known throughout Europe, and she was often complimented for being so zealous. She was never missing from Mass, which was recited in Latin at the time, and she helped to translate some religious works into English. During that time, religion was shrouded in mystery since most texts and all services were conducted in Latin. This made it somewhat inaccessible to the common people, who only spoke English.

Henry VIII and Religion

Despite what Henry VIII did in his later years, he enthusiastically observed the traditional Catholic religion during the beginning of his reign. It's also important to note that Catherine of Aragon was a devout Catholic woman who was related to some of the most powerful Catholic rulers in Europe. Margaret Beaufort also guided

Henry VIII through the beginning weeks of his reign, and it was obvious that she left a powerful mark on her young grandson. Henry VIII took a keen interest in theology and was known for being a benefactor of the church. His support for the church was so powerful and energetic that Pope Leo X gave Henry the title of Defender of the Faith in 1521. Unfortunately, his support wouldn't survive the "Great Matter."

49. The Divorce of Catherine of Aragon

When England first split from the Roman Church, it retained many of the traditional beliefs and practices. However, the Protestant Reformation had begun to take hold in Europe, and those ideas began to filter into England. At first, Henry was dismissive of Protestant beliefs since he didn't put much stock into them, but his mind began to change. While he didn't enthusiastically embrace the new beliefs, he was happy to dissolve the monasteries in 1535. Meanwhile, some of his ministers began the Reformation in earnest. Thomas Cromwell took the lead and was appointed as the king's vice regent in church affairs. He quickly began overturning old traditions and instituted guidelines for the new priests he recruited.

The new clergy aimed to educate their congregations about the seven deadly sins and the Ten Commandments. Cromwell was heavily influenced by the writings of Martin Luther, who rejected many Catholic teachings. What had started as a way to get the king a divorce had become a full-blown Reformation that stunned the Catholic Church.

The Protestant Reformation in Europe

The winds of change began blowing against the Catholic Church in 1517 when a German monk named Martin Luther began challenging the church's teachings. It all started when Martin Luther published his *Ninety-five Theses*, which was a list of topics about Christianity that directly opposed the teachings of the church. One of his biggest grievances was indulgences. At the time, the church sold a certificate that pardoned sins and could be bought in advance. Martin Luther argued that forgiveness was a gift of faith and obedience, not something that could be put up for sale.

50. Martin Luther

He paved the way for splinter groups that broke away from the Catholic Church; they became known as Protestants. Soon, the church was faced with a wave of opposition, as learned men such as John Calvin and Ulrich Zwingli challenged fundamental church practices, such as the Holy Communion. A group called the Anabaptists emerged and argued that baptism should be performed on consenting adults instead of on uncomprehending infants.

In essence, the Catholic Church had presented itself as the intermediary between humans and God for centuries. The only way to get to God was through the church and his chosen representative, the pope. Most of the reforms were aimed at making people less dependent on the church, as Protestants wanted people to be responsible for their own spirituality. This led to radical practices such as distributing the Holy Bible in common languages and the rejection of fundamental Catholic practices.

The New Beliefs

After Martin Luther wrote his *Ninety-five Theses,* he pinned it to the door of his local church. Before long, it spread like wildfire. His ideas about religion were revolutionary and sparked fierce debate throughout the continent. As soon as his *Theses* was published, he began translating the Bible from Latin to German, which enraged the church. For centuries, the clergy was tasked with helping the ordinary people to understand the Bible, which made congregations reliant on the preacher. If people wanted to know anything about religion, God, or the Bible, they had to approach priests, who would then recite church doctrine back at them.

Luther's ideas spread, and before long, the Reformation had begun. The Catholic Church had a serious problem on its hands. While Protestants and Catholics shared the same God, their approach to religion was vastly different. Their vastly differing ideas would lead to vicious conflicts. Protestants believed that saints, pilgrimages, relics, and images were unnecessary and that everyone had a personal responsibility to maintain their faith. This was in direct contrast to the Catholic faith; the things Protestants rejected were fundamental aspects of the Catholic religion. Catholics believed that they needed the church to connect them to God, while the Protestants believed that the Catholic Church was corrupt and keeping people from God.

Relics, in particular, were important to Catholics. They believed that relics were the physical remains of a saint. Anything that was touched or left behind by a saint had holy significance. These artifacts were so important that Catholics would undertake long journeys to pray to relics during times of distress. These journeys were known as pilgrimages. Another key difference between Protestants and Catholics was their ideas about Mass. The Catholics believed in transubstantiation, a process during which the bread and wine became the body and blood of Christ when consumed. Many Protestants rejected the belief in transubstantiation.

Edward VI's Protestant Reforms

Henry VIII may have started the English Reformation, but England only became a Protestant country during Edward VI's reign. The young king had been heavily influenced by his stepmother, Catherine Parr, and his main advisors, Edward Seymour, John Dudley, and Thomas Cranmer. Edward VI was only a boy, but he enthusiastically endorsed Protestantism. While he may not have personally enacted many of the reforms, they were all carried out in his name. During this time, radical reforms had become a reality, as icons, stained glass scenes, and murals were taken out of churches. Church services were conducted in English, priests were allowed to marry, and the saints faded into obscurity.

There were some rebellions against these new reforms, but they were brutally defeated. People were concerned about the sudden and radical changes that were taking place. The English Reformation had moved from debates to drastic actions, which caused instability for the general population. Edward VI's reign saw the destruction of old traditions that had been observed by the people for hundreds of years. Catholic altars were replaced with communion tables, and Catholic icons were removed or destroyed. While the Reformation had been around for a few years already, it had mostly occurred in small pockets in Europe or had been a matter of theoretical debate. However, when Edward VI took the throne, those reforms touched almost every church in the country.

While the young king was greatly influenced by powerful advisors, it was clear that he was a devout Protestant. After all, he made great efforts to keep his Catholic sister, Mary, from the throne.

Thomas Cranmer

Thomas Cranmer was responsible for most of the reforms that took place during Edward VI's reign, and he was the first Protestant archbishop of Canterbury. As the youngest son of a gentleman, it was traditionally accepted that Thomas would join the clergy. However, while studying at Cambridge University, he became a part of the "White Horse" group, which was interested in the Protestant Reformation. Cranmer came into contact with the royal family when he served as Thomas Boleyn's (Anne Boleyn's father) chaplain. Cranmer was instrumental in solving the king's "Great Matter," which launched him to prominence in the Tudor court.

In fact, it was Cranmer who may have planted the idea that Henry VIII should split from the Roman Church. He proposed the idea that the matter of the king's divorce wasn't a legal matter but rather a moral one and that the pope should have no say in the king's divine judgment. Cranmer was eventually made the king's chaplain, and in time, he became the archbishop of Canterbury. For the next few years, Cranmer would be instrumental in obtaining the king's divorce and presided over the king's next marriages.

Cranmer also took the lead in the dissolution of the monasteries and other reforms during Henry VIII's reign, but he would go on to implement more radical changes during Edward VI's reign. In 1547, he released the *First Book of Homilies*, which set the guidelines for how priests should conduct their services. However, his greatest accomplishment was the *Book of Common Prayer.*

The *Book of Common Prayer*

The *Book of Common Prayer* was written by Thomas Cranmer in 1549. It was used during church services and outlined reforms that the church was forced to observe, as the Act of Uniformity made it mandatory for the whole country. The first edition of the book was meant to serve as a bridge between new and old religious ideas. It was supposed to help make the English Reformation more palatable and easier to understand, but it was still a departure from the traditional beliefs. It was purposefully vague on some matters, but it still stirred up opposition since it was too radical for the supporters of the traditional religion and not radical enough for staunch Protestants. Finally, a second edition was released in 1552, which was even more radical than the first and made some clarifications.

For example, the second edition completely rejected the teaching of transubstantiation and angered Catholics. It was the radical changes that the Protestants had wanted, but it also led to opposition and rebellions. The book was an important part of the English Reformation and helped to spread Protestant beliefs. It was a way to impose the Reformation in every church in the country. While the *Book of Common Prayer* was likely one of Cranmer's proudest achievements, it made him even more unpopular with the Catholics. The book also included offensive prayers against the pope, which didn't help its popularity with the Catholics. Unfortunately for Cranmer, his efforts during the English Reformation made him some dangerous enemies, including the next queen of England, Mary I.

Mary I's Return to Rome

While Edward VI and his Protestant advisors tried desperately to keep Mary I from the throne, they vastly underestimated how many people would fight for her. While Lady Jane Grey was a Protestant and would ensure that England remained a Protestant country, Mary I was the legitimate Tudor heir. There were many nobles and commoners who disapproved of the way she had been disinherited, and they were eager to support her rise to the throne. Unfortunately for the Protestants, she immediately began undoing the Reformation and dutifully returned England back to the pope. She was a staunch Catholic, and she had been horrified by what had happened.

In 1553, she removed the *Book of Common Prayer* and returned the old Latin prayer books to the churches. She quickly removed all the reforms that had taken place during her predecessors' reigns. However, the country's return to Catholicism wasn't as popular as she had hoped. For one thing, the nobles weren't eager to return their new lands and relinquish money to the church. Her marriage to a Spanish prince angered the populace. Some people had also become attached to Protestantism, which was a difficult fact for Mary to accept. She wasn't willing to compromise, and after Wyatt's rebellion, she began taking more extreme steps. In 1554, she began burning prominent Protestants. Thomas Cranmer was arrested in 1555.

Cranmer had helped to enact the law that made it treasonous to observe different religious beliefs than the monarch, and he was forced to recant his Protestantism. It was a heavy blow against the Reformation. However, when Cranmer was led to the stake in 1556, he stuck his hand in the fire and claimed that he was burning off the hand that signed his recantation. This action became legendary and turned Cranmer into a Protestant martyr. Unfortunately for Mary I, the English Reformation was far from over.

Elizabeth I and Protestant England

When Elizabeth I became queen in 1558, the country would once again switch religions. However, this time, the transition would be permanent. Elizabeth I was a practical woman and chose not to impose radical reforms on her people. When she became queen, she restored the *Book of Common Prayer* but took out some of the more radical or offensive aspects. She also maintained a strict hierarchy within the church and appointed bishops. Elizabeth had seen what misplaced religious zeal could do to a monarch, so she was much more careful in instituting her reforms. While some people were frustrated by her approach, it was a success. English Protestantism became known as Anglicism.

Chapter 15: Culture and Art

The Tudor dynasty brought about some of the most climatic changes in English history. The Tudor court was filled with dangerous, ambitious individuals who didn't flinch when the country descended into chaos for their own gain. It was an interesting time filled with fascinating characters and deadly conflicts. However, it was also a time of great cultural and artistic changes. Toward the end of the Tudor period, the arts flourished, and the English Renaissance began.

The Tudor court also housed some of the most interesting and famous artists of the time. The royal family's portraits were painted by highly talented individuals, while London was the home of some of the most influential writers of all time. Elizabeth I, in particular, was a great patron of the arts, and under her care, the Renaissance took root in England. Moreover, renowned literary and architectural works were developed during the period, and some of those elements can still be seen in modern society. While the Tudors were gripped in personal, political, and religious turmoil, art became an important and defining feature of the period.

English Renaissance

The English Renaissance began in the latter half of the 15th century and was a result of the Renaissance that had begun earlier in Europe, most notably in Italy. The Wars of the Roses kept England isolated from developments in Europe, especially in regard to its military, but the civil war also restricted cultural innovations. When the Tudors took over, these artistic and cultural aspects were allowed to arrive in England from Europe, but the Renaissance gained the most momentum during Elizabeth I's reign.

While the Italian Renaissance saw great advancements in paintings and sculptures, the English Renaissance was more focused on music and literary works. The English Renaissance mainly took place during the Tudor era, but English literature had been ahead of its time for decades. Writers such as Chaucer popularized writing their works in French while most of Europe still used Latin. However, England was far behind the visual styles that were being used in mainland Europe, and many of their most famous artists had been imported from there. The most notable examples of foreign artists in the Tudor court were Hans Holbein and Levina Teerlinc.

As the Reformation ripped through the country, it also impacted the artists of the time. Icons were banned in England, and as a result, the visual arts of England were focused on portraits and landscapes. A particularly popular form of art was the portrait miniature, which was invented and developed in England. Skilled artists created miniature portraits that could be kept in lockets. This art style became very popular in Europe over time. As time went on, portraits became more intricate, as artists painted symbolic objects meant to convey certain messages to viewers. The *Armada Portrait* painted during Elizabeth I's reign is a prime example of that trend.

51. *Armada Portrait*

Many of Elizabeth I's portraits were filled with symbolic objects. These portraits were usually painted to emphasize the queen's virginity and purity.

Tudor Literature

English authors had built up a reputation for writing their works in the common English language for decades before the English Renaissance began. This would have provided a firm foundation for writers who worked during the Renaissance. The Reformation also helped to popularize the practice of writing in English instead of Latin. For centuries, Latin had been seen as the learned language and was used for many literary works, but the English Renaissance helped to change that trend somewhat. The practice of writing in English also helped to develop the language in terms of structure and grammar. As the Bible was being translated from Latin to English, there were fierce debates about how to capture the essence of the holy writings in a comparatively limited language. In 1526, William Tyndale published his translation of the Bible, which helped develop the English language.

The Tudor princesses, Mary and Elizabeth, received some of the finest education in Europe, which likely influenced Elizabeth's love of theater and literature. One of Elizabeth's tutors, Roger Ascham, was known as the "Father of English Prose." As London's population grew and people began making a lot of money, they found that they wanted entertainment. London's theaters filled that need, which led to the emergence of remarkable plays and playwrights.

Tudor Architecture

One of the most famous Tudor building projects was that of Hampton Palace, which was started in 1515 and built for Thomas Wolsey. However, when Wolsey fell from grace, he gave the palace to Henry VIII to try and appease the king's anger. Wolsey had spent a large amount of money on it with the aim of creating the most beautiful palace in England. This ambition likely contributed to his downfall. The architectural style of this time is known as the Tudor style, and it featured a blend of Gothic and Renaissance styles. Buildings constructed in the Tudor style usually featured intricate decorative brickwork.

52. Hampton Court Palace

During Elizabeth I's reign, the wool trade declined in profitability, which led to a resurgence in farming that helped to enrich many of her subjects. However, this new money didn't motivate the queen to build new palaces or castles. Instead, her nobles built luxurious houses and were required to host the queen during her travels. Country manors were modernized, and government buildings were updated, which led to the emergence of the distinctive Elizabethan style that featured a lot of glass.

Influential Tudor Artists

For much of the Tudor dynasty, foreign artists were employed by the royal court with the express purpose of painting portraits of the royal family and high-ranking nobility. These artists lived in luxury but had the responsibility of painting flattering portraits of their patrons. This kind of lifestyle would have been stressful, and it wouldn't have allowed for a lot of creative freedom. However, several notable people managed to keep royal favor for most of their lives. In some cases, these artists were sent overseas to paint portraits of prospective brides or grooms. This was an important job since there could be dire consequences if it was not done right, as was demonstrated in the case of Henry VIII and Anne of Cleves.

- ## Hans Holbein the Younger

Hans Holbein came from a long line of artists who gained fame and renown in Europe, especially in Germany. Holbein studied under his father and began working by himself in 1515 in Switzerland. During his younger years, he traveled through Europe and developed a distinctive style that helped his career develop. In 1523, he painted a portrait of the famed Dutch scholar Desiderius Erasmus. By 1537, he was officially employed by Henry VIII. He painted portraits of Henry VIII, Jane Seymour, and Anne of Cleves. Holbein was famous for his precise and realistic drawings and paintings, which likely helped to launch him to fame.

- ## Levina Teerlinc

Levina Teerlinc was born around 1520 in Flanders and became one of the most famous miniature portrait painters of her time. It's likely that Levina learned her craft from her father and gained a level of popularity in Flanders before she was invited to work at Henry VIII's court in 1546. She worked hard and rose to prominence within the English royal court and worked for all of Henry VIII's heirs. The fact that she was a favorite in the royal court was evidenced by the fact that she received many expensive gifts from the Tudor monarchs.

- ## Nicholas Hilliard

Nicholas Hilliard was born in 1547 and became one of the most famous English painters during the English Renaissance. He was a particular favorite of Queen Elizabeth I and brought the art of miniature portrait painting to new heights. Hilliard was sent to Geneva as a child to escape the persecution of Protestants but returned by 1559. By 1570, he was working in Queen Elizabeth I's court. Hilliard also had considerable skill as a goldsmith and jeweler. The queen admired his skills so much that she appointed him to design her second great seal.

Tudor Writers

In modern times, English is a complex language with precise rules and thousands of words. However, that wasn't always true, and in the medieval era, English was a simple vernacular language. There weren't many established rules for the language. While there were dedicated schools that taught Latin grammar, English didn't receive the same treatment, as it wasn't seen as the language of learned scholars. In time, this would change. English writers began to develop the language and invented new words. These writers originally came to prominence to satisfy London's growing need for dramatic entertainment, but they ended up creating some of the most influential works in English history.

- ## William Shakespeare

William Shakespeare was one of the most famous and influential writers of his time. He was born in 1564 in Stratford-upon-Avon. Shakespeare came from a humble background and married a local girl named Anne Hathaway when he was eighteen years old. He couldn't stay in the little town forever and went to London in 1592. Shakespeare began to rise quickly and was invited to join Lord Chamberlain's Men, a theater company. Shakespeare's plays were performed at the Globe and featured the relatively famous actor, Richard Burbage. Almost as soon as he began his career as a writer, he began accumulating wealthy friends and patrons who greatly appreciated his writing. By the end of his career, he had written 154 sonnets and about 37 plays.

Shakespeare is famous for the universality and relatability of his works. His works show great wit and perceptiveness that gave them lasting power.

• Edmund Spenser

Edmund Spenser was one of the most famous and influential poets in English history. He was born around 1553 to a noble family that didn't have much money. When he was a teenager, his poems were featured in an anti-Catholic tract commissioned by a rich Flemish man named Jan Baptista van der Noot. When Spenser graduated from grammar school, he attended the University of Cambridge, where he studied literature in various languages.

He learned from epic poets, such as Virgil and others. In time, he wrote the epic poem, *The Faerie Queene*, which later inspired writers like Shakespeare. He lived through some of the most interesting times of the Reformation, and much of his work was influenced by the religious turmoil. Spenser gained a lot of fame for *The Faerie Queene*, which celebrated Elizabeth I's reign, but he was famous in his own right before penning the epic.

• Sir Thomas Wyatt

Sir Thomas Wyatt was born in 1503 and gained attention for his questionable alliances and, more importantly, his highly individualistic poetry. He had been accredited with introducing elements from French and Italian poetry to English literature. Wyatt was known for being an attractive man who gained a lot of attention at Henry VIII's court, where the ideals of medieval chivalry were celebrated. The young nobleman fit the picture of the romantic medieval knight since he was skilled in tournament games, poetry, and music. However, his popularity with women nearly got him executed in 1536 when he was arrested for allegedly having an affair with Anne Boleyn.

Wyatt wrote several poems and sonnets during his lifetime, as well as songs that increased his fame. Unfortunately, he wasn't as gifted at politics and was arrested after his friend Thomas Cromwell was executed. His son would lead the Wyatt rebellion, which got Elizabeth I arrested.

• Henry Howard

Henry Howard was born in 1517 and received a fine education as the son of Lord Thomas Howard. Henry eventually became the duke of Norfolk. He had a prominent position in Henry VIII's court, which may have influenced some of his poetry. He was accredited with creating the foundation for the age of English poetry. During his youth, he was nearly betrothed to Princess Mary, but that betrothal (like so many of her betrothals) fell through. Later, he served in Henry's army in Scotland and France. Unfortunately, his fortune fell when the Seymours took over once Edward VI was appointed as king.

Henry Howard was charged with treason when it was discovered that he was closely allied with Roman Catholics. He was executed at thirty years old but left behind numerous poems that were only published after his death.

• Sir Philip Sidney

Sir Philip Sidney was born in 1554 and is considered to be the ideal gentleman of the Elizabethan era. He also had the distinction of writing one of the best sonnets of the period. Sidney was responsible for introducing many European Renaissance ideas to English literary circles and worked as a statesman in Elizabeth I's court. He studied at Shrewsbury School as a child and later attended Oxford. He spent some time during his younger years traveling around Europe, where he was likely introduced to the themes and ideas that pervaded his works.

Sidney spoke Latin, Italian, and French perfectly, which helped to increase his knowledge and appreciation of European poetry. By his early twenties, Sidney was working in Queen Elizabeth I's court and given serious responsibilities. He had many interests and was friends with some of the most important artists of his time, including Edmund Spenser.

- ### Roger Ascham

Roger Ascham was born around 1515 and became a renowned scholar who had revolutionary theories about education. He was also one of the biggest promoters of the vernacular English language and was known for being a humanist. Humanism focuses on the individual and social potential of all people. It is a philosophy that believes people have the responsibility of conducting moral and philosophical inquiries.

Ascham studied at Cambridge University, where he learned to appreciate the classical Greek writers. He tutored Princess Elizabeth in Greek and Latin while also holding several positions within the Tudor court. He later served as Mary I's Latin secretary. When Elizabeth took the throne, he became her secretary and helped her study Greek. His most famous work, the *Scholemaster*, was published after his death.

Famous Tudor Portraits

Unlike the Italian Renaissance, the English Renaissance wasn't focused on the visual arts. This might be partly due to the fact that during the Reformation, icons were destroyed and discouraged. Icons were associated with the Roman Catholic religion, and many artists didn't want to find themselves on the wrong side of the law, especially since there were other places in Europe where the visual arts were being developed. However, portraits and landscapes were favorites in England. The Tudor era saw the development of portrait painting as an art, and artists eventually focused on symbolism. Some of the most famous portraits during the time were of various members of the royal family.

- The *Portrait of Henry VIII*

While Henry VIII had many portraits of himself commissioned during his reign, one of the most notable portraits is the *Portrait of Henry VIII* by Hans Holbein the Younger. It was painted when Henry was in his forties. The portrait depicts Henry as a younger and healthier version of himself when he was, in reality, old, obese, and grossly afflicted by an ulcerated leg. Holbein's portrait gave Henry the powerful presence that he had long since lost, which enchanted the king. He spread the portrait throughout the kingdom. His nobles had the portrait recreated to please the king. The original was lost in a fire, but since there were so many recreations, we are able to know what it looked like.

53. *Portrait of Henry VIII*

- The Portrait of Jane Seymour

An unfinished portrait of Jane Seymour has been the subject of scholarly curiosity since it depicts the deceased queen and was likely painted soon after her death in 1537. There are various elements in the painting that were never finished, and while it showed distinctive painting styles of the time, it was never completed. It's possible that it was commissioned by the Seymour family but abandoned when they fell from prominence.

• The *Rainbow Portrait* of Queen Elizabeth I

One of the most famous portraits of Elizabeth I is the *Rainbow Portrait*, in which she holds a rainbow, a symbol of peace. No one is sure who painted the portrait, and several artists, including Isaac Oliver, Marcus Gheeraerts the Younger, and Taddeo Zuccari, have been accredited with the painting. While the rainbow symbolizes peace, the queen's dress is embroidered with wildflowers and pearls, which are images associated with the Virgin Mary. The eyes and ears that were painted on her skirt are supposed to remind the viewer that the queen was keenly aware of the needs of her people. Other symbols include a snake, which symbolizes wisdom. The painting hints that her power is as important as the sun to her people.

54. The *Rainbow Portrait*

There's no doubt that the Tudor era ushered in a period of literary and artistic innovation that left its mark on English history and the English language.

Chapter 16: Daily Life in Tudor England

Since the Tudor era was filled with climactic changes, it would be easy to imagine that daily life in the period would be filled with exciting events and strange customs. However, most of the population wasn't affected by the scandalous lives of the royals and nobles. Sometimes, they would have to answer a call to arms or march off to a foreign country to fight in a war, but other than that, life was relatively restful for those who had nothing to do with the noble houses.

Daily life in Tudor England depended greatly on a person's status. There were different rules for the social classes, and a person's rank was displayed through their clothes and food. However, that didn't mean that life was always better for the rich. Many nobles had to live at the royal court, which was a boring and extremely expensive way of life. The poor didn't have things easy either. They had to navigate a biased justice system to eke out a living. While most people weren't directly affected by the changes that occurred in the Tudor era, in time, their ways of life were subtly impacted. This could be seen in church life, entertainment, and the observance of public holidays.

Family Life

Families in Tudor England tended to be larger than most modern families. Parents were encouraged to have as many children as possible. Besides the parents and children, family units usually consisted of grandparents, cousins, servants, and apprentices. If something happened to a person's parents or spouse, they could usually expect to move in with their extended family. Family was an important part of life in Tudor England.

Unfortunately, illness was common, and babies often didn't survive infancy. Living conditions were usually dirty, damp, and overcrowded, which proved to be fatal for young children. There was no distinction between the poor and rich in this regard, and most parents lost at least one child.

The prevalent belief during the time period was that children were born with a natural badness in them. It was the parents' responsibility to discipline the children, which involved beating them. Despite the harsh disciplinary rules of the time, parents cared deeply for their children and often bought or built toys for their little ones.

55. Toy horse constructed sometime after the medieval era

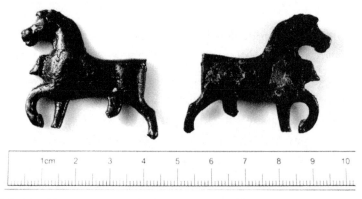

Rich families spent much less time together. As soon as a child in a wealthy family was born, they were handed over to a wetnurse who fed them. The children grew up with tutors or sometimes in other noble houses. Royal children were taken from their parents while they were still babies and received a household to care for their needs. Most princes and princesses never lived with their parents and weren't part of a traditional family unit.

Marriage

There is a common misconception that everyone married young during the Tudor era, but this is untrue. Marriage was commonly viewed as an economical affair rather than having anything to do with love. Rich families usually arranged marriages for their children when they were still young, perhaps even babies. Their primary concern was the economic or social viability of a match. While rich children knew who they would marry by the time they reached puberty, they didn't actually get married until the bride was in her late teens, often until she was about sixteen. This practice was enforced by Margaret Beaufort when she set several acts about marriage and childbirth; this was likely due to her own traumatic experience. For most of English history, this had been an unspoken rule, but she saw the need to make it a spoken one.

Marriage among the lower classes was a much simpler affair. Women usually got married in their mid-twenties, while men waited a little longer. Since life expectancy was shorter during this period, it wasn't uncommon for people to be married a few times during their life. If a man was widowed, he would usually marry as quickly as possible so that his family would be taken care of while he worked. The same was true of widowed women who could still expect to have children. A common practice during the time was for the widow of a tradesman to marry one of her deceased husband's apprentices so that they could keep the business going. In certain cases, a widow past her childbearing years would marry if it was a good economic match, as was the case of Margaret Beaufort's marriage to Lord Thomas Stanley.

Death

Death was a common and unfortunate feature of the Tudor era that usually affected daily life. The beginning of the Tudor era saw the world emerging from the horrors of the Black Death, which had left a definite mark on the common people. They were suddenly tormented by the religious teachings of purgatory and hell since many of them had lost at least one family member to the plague.

The religious teaching of hell stated that people who were judged as sinners would be burned and tortured for the rest of eternity. The teaching of purgatory stated that some people weren't bad enough to warrant hell but weren't good enough to reach heaven either. This meant that they languished until they were cleansed of their sins and allowed to reach heaven. As a result of these teachings, people paid massive sums to have the clergy pray for their family members who might have been trapped in purgatory. It also led to the practice of chantries, where rich people could be buried and prayed for together. Some wealthy families even donated to chapels or built family burial sites on holy ground.

56. Tomb in Beauchamp Chapel

Of course, the church made a lot of money off of death rites, but all that changed during the Reformation. From then on, death rites became more private and were conducted according to a person's conscience.

Holidays

The Tudor era saw the rise of public holidays, which were observed by both the rich and the poor. These were days when people could take a break from normality and let loose. Drinking and merrymaking were common on feast days, and some fun traditions were born. For example, a "king of the feast" would be chosen and paraded around for all to see. Apprentices could roam around the streets and "discipline" their elders by setting ridiculous rules and laws. These traditions were a source of great entertainment. The rich would also impress their social status in their communities by paying for such revelries and giving money to the poor.

Holy days were favorites among the people because they could expect feasts, music, and games, which gave them a well-deserved rest from their daily work. New Years, Christmas, Twelfth Day, Ash Wednesday, Lady Day, Easter, May Day, and Accession Day were all public holidays, but there were many more that had their own customs and traditions.

May Day and Whitsunday were particular favorites since these were summer festivals during which feasts, dancing, and plays were common. While these holidays were a source of joy, they also required a lot of work. Usually, people would begin making food and preparing for the feast the night before the holiday. Sometimes, they would also fast before a holy day, which usually meant they avoided meat. Most people didn't mind, however, as they knew they could look forward to a massive meal the next day.

Life in the Royal Court

The nobility certainly led an easier life than the lower classes, but that didn't mean they enjoyed constant glamor or entertainment. Often, they were called to serve the monarch at court and couldn't leave without express permission from their ruler. They received rooms at court according to their rank and were expected to furnish these rooms and keep their own servants. This was massively expensive since they were expected to display their wealth and only have the finest furniture. Moreover, they were expected to keep up with courtly fashion, which could cost a fortune. Life at court was a constant drain on resources, and many noble families ended up bankrupt after living there.

The royal court was the heart of the nation, especially in regard to politics. Nobles could gain a lot of lands and money if they made their monarch happy, but it could be a boring way of life, as they had to wait for the monarch to make an appearance. Some nobles had important positions, such as on the Privy Council or as the monarch's advisors, while others just lived at court. When the monarch moved to a different palace, the courtiers were expected to pack up and follow them.

Nobles dined together, and there were different spaces for different ranks of nobles. The king's dining rooms were always filled with roasted meat and luxurious dishes. And the Tudor monarchs' palaces were designed like mazes, with the royal family's rooms in the middle. They were surrounded by their favorites, while lower-ranking nobles lived on the outer edges of the maze and rarely saw the monarch.

Entertainment

Entertainment was an important part of Tudor society. There were many different activities to keep people busy, but they usually depended on a person's social standing. Common activities included going to the theater or going to a bear baiting. The latter was a brutal pastime in which a bear was chained to a pole by its neck or leg. Dogs would be released into the arena, and the crowds would watch the ensuing fight with interest.

Music was a popular feature of the era, and people usually gathered together to hear or play music together. Dancing events allowed people to get together to dance and socialize. These events ranged from local dances to noble balls where alliances were created. There were also more casual pastimes, such as board games, gambling, and card games.

The rich had more time than the other classes and were constantly looking to provide the most lavish entertainment for their friends. They would host great feasts and balls with exotic menus. They also used the time to show off their belongings and hired acrobats, jesters, musicians, or jugglers to keep their friends entertained. If they weren't entertaining guests or attending court, they usually kept busy in their gardens or pursued hobbies like painting or music.

The poorer classes usually had Sunday afternoons to themselves or looked forward to public holidays.

Sports

Sports were a popular pastime during the Tudor era. People used to take part in tennis, archery, fencing, bowls (this game is played on a bowling green and involves rolling a large ball toward a stationary object), football (soccer), and hockey. While these games are still played, the Tudor versions were much less refined and could lead to injuries. The richer classes enjoyed pursuits such as hunting or hawking. They kept large lands stocked with deer and other game, which could provide hours of entertainment. Trained hawks were also used in hunting expeditions. Unfortunately, nobles often closed off large pieces of land for their hunting and restricted their access to the common people. They also persecuted poachers harshly.

Fishing was enjoyed by all classes, but it was mostly pursued by the rich as a hobby. Some poorer people relied on fishing as an extra source of food. Lawn games became especially popular during the Elizabethan era, and nobles were often seen playing bowls or lawn tennis. These games were usually reserved for the rich since they required a lot of time and expensive equipment.

More leisurely pastimes included reading and needlework, the latter of which was always reserved for women. Meanwhile, men would engage in more rowdy games, such as hot cockles or blind man's bluff. The first game, hot cockles, involved one player putting his head in the lap of another player. Then, the other players would take turns slapping his rear end. The first player could only leave the lap if he correctly guessed who hit him last.

Chess, draughts, and checkers were also popular at the time, as was gambling, which led to a lot of fighting.

Tournaments and Masques

Tournaments and jousts remained a popular pastime for the aristocracy. While the Tudor era progressed, armor and knights became obsolete, as wars were fought with guns, warships, and cannons instead. Still, the practice of jousting was still a fun activity for the rich. These tournaments were usually accompanied by other entertainment, such as performers, musicians, and feasts. Tournaments also featured many militaristic elements to delight the crowd. Soldiers, such as pikemen and archers, usually showed off their skills to the public, which served as military propaganda and entertainment. Archery and knife throwing were popular games during festivals and tournaments, and the people could usually take part in some of the games.

57. Jousting

In time, fencing became more popular than jousting, as it was a safer and more sophisticated sport. While tournaments and festivals were usually public affairs, and common people could sometimes enjoy these pastimes, masques were part of the entertainment hosted only by the royal court. Masques were pageants where nobles could show off their singing, dancing, and acting skills. These events usually had themes, storylines, or recreations that involved different characters dressed in rich costumes. They were meant to emphasize the luxury and sophistication of the royal court. The monarch was usually featured in a prominent role.

Henry VIII, in particular, enjoyed participating in masques and presenting himself as a knight from medieval romantic literature. Masques were popular in European royal courts and were an important part of courtly life, especially during Henry VIII's reign. Sometimes, these masques featured allegorical content and were very dramatic, which delighted everyone involved.

A Trip to the Theater

The theater industry boomed during Elizabeth I's reign. Her reign signified the height of the English Renaissance, and she was the patron of several influential playwrights. During this time, actors became famous, and dramatic plays were developed to please the crowds. The theater entertained people of all classes, and everyone was welcome, although some theaters were exclusively for the rich.

The Globe was one of the most famous theaters of its time and featured many of Shakespeare's plays.

At first, actors were part of traveling troupes who went from village to village all throughout the kingdom, but as the troupes made more money, they were able to stay in one place. This allowed them to put more money into their costumes and sets, which heightened the quality of their performances. Some theaters put on daily plays. In the past, plays were mostly recreations of religious events, but in the Tudor era, plays were about history, revenge, murder, romance, comedy, and tragedy. This new form of art thrilled the poor and rich alike, and they eagerly lined up to watch this exciting form of entertainment.

All-purpose theaters were built in London and were simple buildings with a stage and seats for the poor and rich. Nobles sponsored actors and playwrights alike, which meant that a lot of money was pouring into the industry. This allowed more people to become actors and playwrights. As the Elizabethan era progressed, incredible talent was revealed and nurtured. One thing was for sure; going to the theater was a treat for all classes during the closing years of the Tudor era.

Conclusion

The Tudor era is one of the most fascinating periods in English history. It featured scandalous monarchs and ambitious individuals who changed their country forever. While the Tudors made powerful enemies in the Catholic Church, they held out against invasion and helped England out of the dark ages that were the Wars of the Roses. Since their antics are the source of much study and debate, it is clear that the Tudors deserve their place in history.

While the Tudors inherited a country that had been ravaged by civil war, by the end of the Tudor era, England had experienced a cultural renaissance and had an advanced fleet at its disposal. Henry VII produced two male heirs and left behind an economically stable country, but his heir would struggle in his own search for an heir and cause incredible instability that saw the total reformation of the church. In the end, the Tudor line died out with a woman who chose to remain single so that she could keep her power intact. It wasn't an easy choice, and she was pressured to find a husband, but she remained firm and became one of the greatest monarchs in English history.

This compelling book took a thorough tour of the era, beginning with an overview of what England was like before the Tudors took power. England was ruled by the Plantagenet dynasty, which was marked by either great or completely ineffectual kings. The country saw glory under kings such as Henry V, but in just a few short years, it was plunged into chaos under a weak king, Henry VI. The Wars of the Roses began during this period and led to vicious fighting that wiped out most of the noble families in the country. These years weren't an easy time for anybody, and the country stalled in terms of innovation and development. Greedy, ambitious nobles ripped their country apart for whatever power they could find, while crafty politicians used their wits to thrive. Out of this chaos, Margaret Beaufort emerged as a victor. She started off as a traumatized young girl with a boy whose life was in constant danger, but she elevated her son to the throne of England. This period also produced tragic stories, such as the princes who were lost in the Tower of London. The Wars of the Roses were brutal, and many people died in the effort to find a true king.

The second section discussed the Tudor monarchs. Henry VII was the first Tudor king, and he was dramatically crowned on the battlefield after defeating the Lancastrian king, Richard III. He united the warring Houses of York and Lancaster and brought peace to the country. Unfortunately, his years in exile left a mark on him, and he suffered a difficult reign marked by treason and rebellion. He faced tragedy when his firstborn died. The throne was then thrust on the young Henry VIII. Despite the promising early years of his reign, Henry VIII became an obese, sickly man who disinherited his daughters and killed or divorced his wives when they made him unhappy. He plunged his country into the English Reformation that was continued by his son, Edward VI.

The Boy King inherited the throne at only nine years old, but he was ruled by ambitious men who were willing to use a child for their own gains. As a devout Protestant, Edward supported the Reformation, but an early death saw the undoing of all his hard work when his Catholic half-sister took the throne. Mary I had been the apple of her father's eye but was cast off when her mother didn't produce a son. Ever since then, she had lived in obscurity and humiliation as everything was stripped away from her. When her time on the throne finally came, she gleefully undid the Reformation but faced backlash from her own people and died alone from a painful disease. Finally, Elizabeth I took the throne. She restarted the Reformation, led her country into the English Renaissance, and fought off the Spanish Armada.

The third section discussed the military and wars that took place during the Tudor era. Henry VII wasn't very interested in war after spending his life fighting to take the throne, but Henry VIII enthusiastically brought his army out of the dark ages with the help of foreign mercenaries. He also built up the navy, which his daughter used to great success against the Spanish.

Finally, the last section dealt with daily life in the Tudor era. Aspects such as politics, religion, society, and culture were discussed in great detail. Life in Tudor England wasn't always peaceful, and society was biased against the poor, but there were also fun occasions that people could look forward to.

The Tudor era was filled with highs and lows, as well as immense changes. The Tudors led their people through foreign wars, a religious reformation, and a cultural renaissance. They truly left behind a unique and enduring legacy.

Here's another book by Enthralling History that you might like

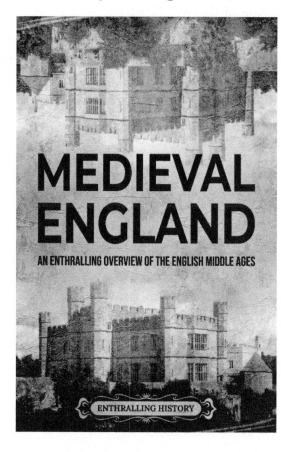

Free limited time bonus

Stop for a moment. We have a free bonus set up for you. The problem is this: we forget 90% of everything that we read after 7 days. Crazy fact, right? Here's the solution: we've created a printable, 1-page pdf summary for this book that you're reading now. All you have to do to get your free pdf summary is to go to the following website: **https://livetolearn.lpages.co/enthrallinghistory/**

Once you do, it will be intuitive. Enjoy, and thank you!

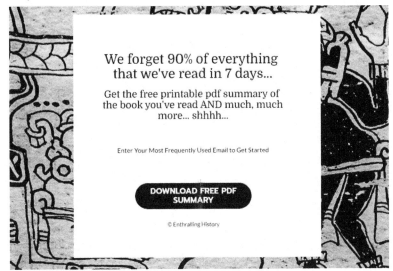

Bibliography

Information Sources

• Link: https://www.britannica.com/topic/house-of-Plantagenet
Date Accessed: 7/2/22
Title: House of Plantagenet

• Link: https://www.englishmonarchs.co.uk/plantagenet_18.htm
Date Accessed: 7/2/22
Title: Plantagenet Kings and Queens

• Link: https://www.britannica.com/biography/Henry-II-king-of-England
Date Accessed: 7/2/22
Title: Henry II

• Link: https://www.historic-uk.com/HistoryUK/HistoryofEngland/King-Henry-II-of-England/
Date Accessed: 7/2/22
Title: King Henry II

• Link: https://www.britannica.com/biography/Richard-I-king-of-England

Date Accessed: 7/2/22

Title: Richard I

• Link: https://www.english-heritage.org.uk/learn/story-of-england/medieval/

Date Accessed: 7/2/22

Title: An Introduction to Medieval England (1066-1485)

• Link: https://www.worldhistory.org/article/1504/the-wars-of-the-roses-consequences--effects/

Date Accessed: 7/2/22

Title: The Wars of the Roses: Consequences & Effects

• Link: https://www.britainexpress.com/History/Knights_and_Fights.htm

Date Accessed: 7/2/22

Title: Medieval Knights and Warfare

• Link: https://www.bl.uk/medieval-literature/articles/love-and-chivalry-in-the-middle-ages

Date Accessed: 7/2/22

Title: Love and Chivalry in the Middle Ages

• Link: https://www.britannica.com/topic/Magna-Carta

Date Accessed: 7/2/22

Title: Magna Carta

• Link: https://dbpedia.org/page/Anglo-French_War_(1213%E2%80%931214)

Date Accessed: 8/2/22

Title: Anglo-French War (1213-1214)

• Link: https://www.worldhistory.org/Henry_III_of_England/

Date Accessed: 8/2/22

Title: Henry III of England

• Link: https://www.worldhistory.org/Edward_I_of_England/

Date Accessed: 8/2/22

Title: Edward I of England

• Link:
https://www.worldhistory.org/Edward_II_of_England/
Date Accessed: 8/2/22
Title: Edward II of England

• Link: https://englishhistory.net/tudor/genealogy-chart-family-tree/
Date Accessed: 8/2/22
Title: House of Tudor Genealogy Chart & Family Tree

• Link:
https://www.worldhistory.org/Edward_III_of_England/
Date Accessed: 8/2/22
Title: Edward III of England

• Link: https://www.britannica.com/biography/Edward-III-king-of-England
Date Accessed: 8/2/22
Title: Edward III

• Link: https://www.worldhistory.org/Hundred_Years'_War/
Date Accessed: 8/2/22
Title: Hundred Years' War

• Link: https://www.britannica.com/topic/house-of-York
Date Accessed: 8/2/22
Title: House of York

• Link: https://www.britannica.com/topic/house-of-Lancaster
Date Accessed: 8/2/22
Title: house of Lancaster

• Link: https://www.britannica.com/topic/Valois-dynasty
Date Accessed: 8/2/22
Title: Valois Dynasty

• Link: https://www.worldhistory.org/Owen_Tudor/
Date Accessed: 8/2/22
Title: Owen Tudor

- Link: https://www.britannica.com/biography/Catherine-of-Valois

Date Accessed: 8/2/22

Title: Catherine of Valois

- Link: https://www.britannica.com/biography/Jasper-Tudor-duke-of-Bedford

Date Accessed: 8/2/22

Title: Jasper Tudor, duke of Bedford

- Link: https://www.tudorsociety.com/edmund-tudor-1st-earl-of-richmond/

Date Accessed: 8/2/22

Title: Edmund Tudor, 1st Earl of Richmond

- Link: https://www.anglesey-history.co.uk/places/penmynydd/index.html

Date Accessed: 10/2/22

Title: Penmynydd-birthplace of royalty

- Link: https://www.history.com/topics/british-history/wars-of-the-roses

Date Accessed: 10/2/22

Title: Wars of the Roses

- Link: https://www.britannica.com/biography/Richard-Neville-16th-earl-of-Warwick

Date Accessed: 10/2/22

Title: Richard Neville, 16th earl of Warwick

- Link: https://www.britannica.com/biography/Edward-IV-king-of-England

Date Accessed: 10/2/22

Title: Edward IV

- Link: https://www.britannica.com/biography/Richard-III-king-of-England

Date Accessed: 10/2/22

Title: Richard III

• Link:
https://soundideas.pugetsound.edu/cgi/viewcontent.cgi?articl
e=1015&context=summer_research
Date Accessed: 10/2/22
Title: The Queens' Blood: A Study of Family Ties during
the Wars of the Roses
• Link: https://www.history.co.uk/articles/margaret-beaufort-
the-kingmaker-and-mother-of-the-tudor-dynasty
Date Accessed: 10/2/22
Title: The Kingmaker Margaret Beaufort: Mother of the
Tudor Dynasty
• Link: https://www.historic-
uk.com/HistoryUK/HistoryofEngland/The-Princes-in-the-
Tower/
Date Accessed: 10/2/22
Title: The Princes in the Tower
• Link: https://www.history.com/this-day-in-history/battle-of-
bosworth-field
Date Accessed: 10/2/22
Title: Battle of Bosworth Field
• Link:
https://www.worldhistory.org/Henry_VII_of_England/
Date Accessed: 16/2/22
Title: Henry VII of England
• Link: https://www.britannica.com/biography/Henry-VII-
king-of-England
Date Accessed: 16/2/22
Title: Henry VII
• Link: https://www.historylearningsite.co.uk/tudor-
england/henry-vii-the-
man/#:~:text=His%20spirit%20was%20distinguished%2C%2
0wise,was%20not%20devoid%20of%20scholarship.
Date Accessed: 20/2/22

Title: Henry VII- the man

- Link: https://www.britannica.com/biography/Henry-VIII-king-of-England

Date Accessed: 21/2/22

Title: Henry VIII

- Link: https://www.worldhistory.org/Henry_VIII_of_England/

Date Accessed: 21/2/22

Title: Henry VIII of England

- Link: https://www.history.com/news/henry-viii-wives

Date Accessed: 21/2/22

Title: Who Were the Six Wives of Henry VIII

- Link: https://www.historyextra.com/period/tudor/henry-six-wives-guide-who-were-they-how-many-spouse-catherine-aragon-anne-boleyn-jane-seymour-anne-cleves-howard-parr-facts/

Date Accessed: 21/2/22

Title: Henry VIII's six wives: your guide to the Tudor king's queen consorts

- Link: https://www.historyextra.com/period/tudor/prince-arthur-catherine-katherine-aragon-king-henry-viii-marriage-death-brother/

Date Accessed: 21/2/22

Title: Prince Arthur, Catherine of Aragon, and Henry VIII: a story of early Tudor triumph and tragedy

- Link: https://www.worldhistory.org/English_Reformation/

Date Accessed: 21/2/22

Title: English Reformation

- Link: https://www.britannica.com/topic/Protestantism/The-Reformation-in-England-and-Scotland

Date Accessed: 21/2/22

Title: The Reformation in England and Scotland

- Link: https://www.britannica.com/biography/Edward-VI

Date Accessed: 21/2/22

Title: Edward VI

- Link: https://www.encyclopedia.com/people/history/british-and-irish-history-biographies/edward-vi

Date Accessed: 21/2/22

Title: Edward VI (England) (1537-1553; Ruled 1547-1553)

- Link: https://www.thehistorypress.co.uk/articles/catherine-parr-henry-viii-s-last-love/

Date Accessed: 21/2/22

Title: Catherine Parr: Henry VIII's Last Love

- Link: https://www.britannica.com/biography/Edward-Seymour-1st-Duke-of-Somerset

Date Accessed: 21/2/22

Title: Edward Seymour, 1ˢᵗ duke of Somerset

- Link: https://www.britannica.com/biography/John-Dudley-duke-of-Northumberland

Date Accessed: 21/2/22

Title: John Dudley, duke of Northumberland

- Link: https://www.britannica.com/biography/Catherine-Parr

Date Accessed: 22/2/22

Title: Catherine Parr

- Link: http://www.luminarium.org/encyclopedia/edwardtoparr1548.htm

Date Accessed: 22/2/22

Title: King Edward VI to Queen Katharine Parr 1547

- Link: https://www.britannica.com/biography/Mary-I

Date Accessed: 22/2/22

Title: Mary I

- Link:https://www.worldhistory.org/Mary_I_of_England/#:
~:text=Mary%20I%20of%20England%20reigned,her%20nic
kname%20'Bloody%20Mary'.
Date Accessed: 22/2/22
Title: Mary I of England
- Link: https://www.englishmonarchs.co.uk/tudor_23.html
Date Accessed: 22/2/22
Title: Philip II of Spain
- Link: https://www.historic-
uk.com/HistoryUK/HistoryofEngland/Lady-Jane-Grey/
Date Accessed: 22/2/22
Title: Lady Jane Grey
- Link: https://www.britannica.com/biography/Elizabeth-I
Date Accessed: 24/2/22
Title: Elizabeth I
- Link:
https://www.worldhistory.org/Elizabeth_I_of_England/
Date Accessed: 24/2/22
Title: Elizabeth I of England
- Link:
https://courses.lumenlearning.com/britlit1/chapter/english-
renaissance/
Date Accessed: 24/2/22
Title: English Renaissance
- Link: https://www.worldhistory.org/Wyatt_Rebellion/
Date Accessed: 24/2/22
Title: Wyatt Rebellion
- Link:
https://www.worldhistory.org/Robert_Dudley_1st_Earl_of_L
eicester/
Date Accessed: 24/2/22
Title: Robert Dudley, 1ˢᵗ Earl of Leicester

- Link:
https://www.worldhistory.org/Mary_Queen_of_Scots/#:~:tex
t=She%20was%20the%20daughter%20of,country%20in%20
her%20own%20right.
Date Accessed: 25/2/22
Title: Mary, Queen of Scots
- Link: https://www.britishbattles.com/wars-of-the-roses/first-
battle-of-st-albans/
Date Accessed: 25/2/22
Title: First Battle of St. Albans
- Link: https://www.historic-
uk.com/HistoryMagazine/DestinationsUK/The-Battle-of-
Stoke-Field/
Date Accessed: 25/2/22
Title: Battle of Stoke Field
- Link: https://www.britishbattles.com/anglo-scottish-
war/battle-of-flodden/
Date Accessed: 25/2/22
Title: Battle of Flodden
- Link: https://www.henryviiithereign.co.uk/1513-battle-of-
spurs.html
Date Accessed: 25/2/22
Title: The Battle of the Spurs
- Link: https://warfarehistorynetwork.com/2016/06/17/king-
henry-viii-england-siege-of-boulogne-his-last-war/
Date Accessed: 25/2/22
Title: King Henry VIII of England and the Siege of
Boulogne: His Last War
- Link: https://www.historic-
uk.com/HistoryUK/HistoryofEngland/The-Great-French-
Armada-of-1545-The-Battle-of-The-Solent/
Date Accessed: 25/2/22

Title: The Great French Armada of 1545 & the Battle of the Solent
- Link: https://www.battlefieldstrust.com/resource-centre/medieval/battleview.asp?BattleFieldId=40

Date Accessed: 25/2/22

Title: Battle of Solway Moss
- Link:https://www.battlefieldstrust.com/resource-centre/medieval/battleview.asp?BattleFieldId=72

Date Accessed: 25/2/22

Title: Battle of Ancrum Moor
- Link:https://www.battlefieldstrust.com/resource-centre/medieval/battleview.asp?BattleFieldId=68

Date Accessed: 25/2/22

Title: Battle of Pinkie
- Link:http://historicaltriumphsanddisasters.blogspot.com/2015/12/england-loses-calais1558.html

Date Accessed: 25/2/22

Title: England loses Calais, 1558
- Link: https://www.historic-uk.com/HistoryUK/HistoryofEngland/Spanish-Armada/

Date Accessed: 25/2/22

Title: The Spanish Armada
- Link: https://www.english-heritage.org.uk/learn/story-of-england/medieval/war/

Date Accessed: 26/2/22

Title: Medieval: Warfare
- Link: https://www.historic-uk.com/HistoryUK/HistoryofEngland/The-Wars-of-the-Roses/

Date Accessed: 26/2/22

Title: The Wars of the Roses
- Link: https://www.britishbattles.com/wars-of-the-roses/battle-of-bosworth-field/

Date Accessed: 26/2/22

Title: Battle of Bosworth Field

- Link: https://www.jstor.org/stable/3816474

Date Accessed: 26/2/22

Title: Notes on the Organization and Supply of the Tudor Military under Henry VII

- Link: https://www.jstor.org/stable/44230050

Date Accessed: 26/2/22

Title: The Army of Henry VIII: A Reassessment

- Link: https://core.ac.uk/download/pdf/30695522.pdf

Date Accessed: 26/2/22

Title: The military obligations of the English people 1511-1558

- Link: https://www.english-heritage.org.uk/about-us/our-places/forts-and-defences/

Date Accessed: 26/2/22

Title: Forts and Defenses

- Link: https://www.rmg.co.uk/stories/topics/henry-viii-his-navy

Date Accessed: 26/2/22

Title: Henry VIII and his navy

- Link: https://maryrose.org/the-history-of-the-mary-rose/

Date Accessed: 26/2/22

Title: The History of the Mary Rose- 1510-1545

- Link: https://www.thehistorypress.co.uk/articles/queen-elizabeth-i-s-sea-dogs/

Date Accessed: 26/2/22

Title: Queen Elizabeth I's Sea Dogs

- Link: https://www.medievalchronicles.com/medieval-weapons/tudor-weapons/#:~:text=The%20conventional%20weapons%20used%20during,%2C%20matchlock%2C%20flintlock%20and%20canons.

Date Accessed: 28/2/22

Title: Tudor Weapons

• Link: https://www.medievalchronicles.com/medieval-history/medieval-history-periods/tudor-england/tudor-weapons-list/

Date Accessed: 28/2/22

Title: Tudor Weapons List

• Link: http://myarmoury.com/feature_armies_eng.html

Date Accessed: 28/2/22

Title: Renaissance Armies: The English- Henry VIII to Elizabeth

• Link: https://www.warhistoryonline.com/history/military-reforms-of-king-henry.html?chrome=1

Date Accessed: 28/2/22

Title: Military Reforms of King Henry the Eighth- He Built Up a Modern Fighting Force in Medieval England

• Link: https://www.medievalchronicles.com/medieval-armour/tudor-armour/

Date Accessed: 28/2/22

Title: Tudor Armour

• Link: https://www.britannica.com/topic/Landsknechte

Date Accessed: 28/2/22

Title: Landsknecht

• Link: https://www.britannica.com/topic/Yeomen-of-the-Guard

Date Accessed: 28/2/22

Title: Yeomen of the Guard

• Link: https://hsu.edu/uploads/pages/2003-4afthedeathof_the_knight.pdf

Date Accessed: 28/2/22

Title: The Death of the Knight: Changes in Military Weaponry during the Tudor Period

- Link:
http://home.mysoul.com.au/graemecook/Renaissance/06_E
nglish.htm
Date Accessed: 28/2/22
Title: Part 6: Henry VIII's Army
- Link: https://www.jstor.org/stable/2639241
Date Accessed: 28/2/22
Title: Review: Politics and Government in Tudor England
- Link: https://www.gale.com/intl/essays/david-j-crankshaw-
tudor-privy-council-c-1540%E2%80%931603
Date Accessed: 28/2/22
Title: The Tudor Privy Council, c. 1540-1603
- Link:
https://www.hoddereducation.co.uk/media/Documents/Hist
ory/AQA_A-
level_History_My_Revision_Notes_The_Tudors_sample_p
ages.pdf
Date Accessed: 28/2/22
Title: The Tudors, England, 1485-1603
- Link: https://www.jstor.org/stable/2594614
Date Accessed: 28/2/22
Title: Population Change, Enclosure, and the Early Tudor
Economy
- Link: https://spartacus-
educational.com/TUDagriculture.htm
Date Accessed: 1/3/22
Title: Agriculture and Enclosures
- Link: https://tudortimes.co.uk/politics-economy/the-
english-wool-trade/economics-of-sheep-farming
Date Accessed: 1/3/22
Title: The English Wool Trade
- Link: https://www.historylearningsite.co.uk/tudor-
england/henry-vii-and-trade/

Date Accessed: 1/3/22

Title: Henry VII and Trade

• Link: https://www.parliament.uk/about/living-heritage/evolutionofparliament/originsofparliament/birthofparliament/overview/reformation/#:~:text=Henry%20VIII's%20Reformation%20Parliament%2C%20which,Papacy%20in%20Rome%20was%20blocking.

Date Accessed: 1/3/22

Title: Reformation Parliament

• Link: https://www.jstor.org/stable/10.1086/339721

Date Accessed: 1/3/22

Title: An Economic Analysis of the Protestant Reformation

• Link: http://elizabethanenglandlife.com/thetudorsfacts/tudor-times-exploration-of-the-world.html

Date Accessed: 1/3/22

Title: Tudor Times Exploration of the World

• Link: https://www.history.org.uk/student/module/4536/overview-of-elizabeth-i/4543/social-structure#:~:text=Elizabethan%20England%20had%20four%20main,and%20their%20children%20could%20get.

Date Accessed: 1/3/22

Title: Social Structure

• Link: https://www.museumoflondon.org.uk/Resources/learning/targettudors/education/theme.html

Date Accessed: 1/3/22

Title: Education: hard work and little play!

• Link: https://www.mylearning.org/stories/the-painted-lady--tudor-portraits-at-the-ferens/254#:~:text=the%20Sumptuary%20Law.-

,Sumptuary%20Law,%2C%20food%2C%20furniture%2C%2
0etc.
Date Accessed: 1/3/22
Title: A Passion for Fashion
• Link: https://tudortimes.co.uk/people/nobility
Date Accessed: 1/3/22
Title: Nobility
• Link: https://www.rmg.co.uk/stories/topics/tudor-
fashion#:~:text=Rich%20men%20wore%20white%20silk,we
re%20fashionable%20throughout%20the%20period.
Date Accessed: 1/3/22
Title: Tudor Fashion
• Link: https://www.hrp.org.uk/hampton-court-
palace/history-and-stories/tudor-food-and-
eating/#:~:text=Food%20for%20a%20King&text=Dishes%2
0included%20game%2C%20roasted%20or,which%20he%20
ate%20sweet%20preserves.
Date Accessed: 1/3/22
Title: Tudor Food and Eating
• Link: https://www.historic-uk.com/CultureUK/Tudor-
Guide-To-Getting-Dressed/
Date Accessed: 1/3/22
Title: A Tudor Guide to Getting Dressed
• Link:
http://www.durhamrecordoffice.org.uk/article/10861/Tudor-
Jobs
Date Accessed: 1/3/22
Title: Tudor Jobs
• Link: https://www.hrp.org.uk/hampton-court-
palace/history-and-stories/life-at-the-tudor-
court/#:~:text=In%20the%201500s%2C%20a%20monarch's,
pleasure%20palace%20and%20a%20hotel.
Date Accessed: 1/3/22

Title: Life at the Tudor Court

• Link: https://www.nationalgeographic.org/article/protestant-reformation/#:~:text=The%20Protestant%20Reformation%20began%20in,people%20to%20debate%20with%20him.

Date Accessed: 3/3/22

Title: The Protestant Reformation

• Link: https://www.english-heritage.org.uk/learn/story-of-england/tudors/religion/#:~:text=But%20although%20Henry%20had%20rejected,radically%20Protestant%20Edward%20VI%20(r.

Date Accessed: 3/3/22

Title: Tudors: Religion

• Link: https://www.worldhistory.org/Thomas_Cranmer/

Date Accessed: 3/3/22

Title: Thomas Cranmer

• Link: https://www.britannica.com/topic/Book-of-Common-Prayer

Date Accessed: 3/3/22

Title: *Book of Common Prayer*

• Link: https://www.newadvent.org/cathen/02376a.htm

Date Accessed: 3/3/22

Title: Lady Margaret Beaufort

• Link: https://www.mylearning.org/stories/tudor-clothing--dress-to-impress/406?

Date Accessed: 3/3/22

Title: What to Look for in Tudor Paintings

• Link: https://www.infoplease.com/encyclopedia/arts/english-lit/20th-century-plus/english-literature/the-tudors-and-the-elizabethan-age#:~:text=A%20myriad%20of%20new%20genres,of%20Surrey%2C%20a%20seminal%20influence.

Date Accessed: 3/3/22

Title: English literature: The Tudors and the Elizabethan Age

• Link: https://courses.lumenlearning.com/britlit1/chapter/english-renaissance/

Date Accessed: 3/3/22

Title: English Renaissance

• Link: https://www.thespruce.com/tudor-architecture-4788228

Date Accessed: 3/3/22

Title: What is Tudor Architecture

• Link: https://www.britannica.com/biography/Hans-Holbein-the-Younger

Date Accessed: 3/3/22

Title: Hans Holbein the Younger

• Link: https://www.encyclopedia.com/women/encyclopedias-almanacs-transcripts-and-maps/teerlinc-levina-c-1520-1576

Date Accessed: 3/3/22

Title: Teerlinc, Levina (c. 1520-1576)

• Link: https://www.britannica.com/biography/Nicholas-Hilliard

Date Accessed: 3/3/22

Title: Nicholas Hilliard

• Link: https://www.britannica.com/biography/William-Shakespeare

Date Accessed: 3/3/22

Title: William Shakespeare

• Link: https://www.britannica.com/biography/Edmund-Spenser

Date Accessed: 3/3/22

Title: Edmund Spenser

- Link: https://www.britannica.com/biography/Thomas-Wyatt

Date Accessed: 3/3/22

Title: Sir Thomas Wyatt

- Link: https://www.britannica.com/biography/Henry-Howard-Earl-of-Surrey

Date Accessed: 3/3/22

Title: Henry Howard, Earl of Surrey

- Link: https://www.britannica.com/biography/Philip-Sidney

Date Accessed: 3/3/22

Title: Sir Philip Sidney

- Link: https://www.britannica.com/biography/Roger-Ascham

Date Accessed: 3/3/22

Title: Roger Ascham

- Link: https://joyofmuseums.com/museums/europe/spain-museums/madrid-museums/thyssen-bornemisza-museum/portrait-of-henry-viii-of-england-by-hans-holbein-the-younger-2/

Date Accessed: 3/3/22

Title: "Portrait of Henry VIII of England" by Hans Holbein the Younger

- Link: https://thetudortravelguide.com/2019/10/19/jane-seymour/

Date Accessed: 3/3/22

Title: Jane Seymour: The Unfinished Portrait of a Tudor Queen

- Link: https://www.worldhistory.org/image/12314/elizabeth-i-rainbow-portrait/

Date Accessed: 3/3/22

Title: Elizabeth I Rainbow Portrait

- Link: https://www.worldhistory.org/article/1581/holidays-in-the-elizabethan-era/

Date Accessed: 4/3/22

Title: Holidays in the Elizabethan Era

• Link: https://www.worldhistory.org/article/1579/sports-games--entertainment-in-the-elizabethan-era/

Date Accessed: 4/3/22

Title: Sports, Games & Entertainment in the Elizabethan Era

• Link: https://www.worldhistory.org/article/1583/education-in-the-elizabethan-era/

Date Accessed: 4/3/22

Title: Education in the Elizabethan Era

• Link: https://www.worldhistory.org/Elizabethan_Theatre/

Date Accessed: 4/3/22

Title: Elizabethan Theatre

• Link: https://www.hrp.org.uk/hampton-court-palace/history-and-stories/life-at-the-tudor-court/

Date Accessed: 4/3/22

Title: Life at the Tudor Court

• Link: https://tudortimes.co.uk/daily-life/family-life

Date Accessed: 4/3/22

Title: Family Life

• Link: https://tudortimes.co.uk/daily-life/death-rites

Date Accessed: 4/3/22

Title: Death Rites

• Link: https://tudortimes.co.uk/daily-life/pastimes

Date Accessed: 4/3/22

Title: Pastimes

• Link: https://tudortimes.co.uk/daily-life/daily-life-objects

Date Accessed: 4/3/22

Title: Objects in Daily Life

• Link:
https://www.museumoflondon.org.uk/Resources/learning/targettudors/family/theme.html#:~:text=Tudor%20families%20

were%20generally%20larger,as%20part%20of%20the%20fa
mily.

Date Accessed: 4/3/22

Title: Family Life: the more the merrier!

• Link: https://www.penguin.co.uk/articles/2017/a-day-in-
the-life-of-a-tudor-courtier.html

Date Accessed: 4/3/22

Title: A day in the life of a Tudor Courtier by Simon
Thurley

Picture Sources

1. Public Domain;
https://commons.wikimedia.org/wiki/File:King_Henry_II_E
ngland.jpg
2. Public Domain;
https://commons.wikimedia.org/wiki/File:Merry-
Joseph_Blondel_-_Richard_I_the_Lionheart.jpg
3. Public Domain;
https://commons.wikimedia.org/wiki/File:Edward_I_-
_Westminster_Abbey_Sedilia.jpg.
4. Public Domain;
https://commons.wikimedia.org/wiki/File:King_Edward_III
_from_NPG.jpg
5. Credit: Sodacan, CC BY-SA 3.0
https://creativecommons.org/licenses/by-sa/3.0 via
Wikimedia Commons;
6. https://commons.wikimedia.org/wiki/File:Red_Rose_Bad
ge_of_Lancaster.svg.
7. Credit: Sodacan This W3C-unspecified vector image was
created with Inkscape., CC BY-SA 3.0
https://creativecommons.org/licenses/by-sa/3.0 via
Wikimedia Commons;

https://commons.wikimedia.org/wiki/File:White_Rose_Badge_of_York.svg.
8. Credit: Wdcf, CC BY-SA 3.0 https://creativecommons.org/licenses/by-sa/3.0 via Wikimedia Commons; https://commons.wikimedia.org/wiki/File:House_of_Tudor.png.
9. Public Domain; https://commons.wikimedia.org/wiki/File:Meynnart_Wewyck_Lady_Margaret_Beaufort.jpg
10. Public Domain; https://commons.wikimedia.org/wiki/File:Battle_Near_Towton_bw.jpg.
11. Public Domain; https://commons.wikimedia.org/wiki/File:Richard_Plantagenet,_3rd_Duke_of_York_2.jpg.
12. Public Domain; https://commons.wikimedia.org/wiki/File:Warwick_the_Kingmaker.gif.
13. Public Domain; https://commons.wikimedia.org/wiki/File:Princes.jpg.
14. Public Domain; https://commons.wikimedia.org/wiki/File:Enrique_VII_de_Inglaterra,_por_un_artista_an%C3%B3nimo.jpg.
15. Public Domain; https://commons.wikimedia.org/wiki/File:Elizabeth_of_York.jpg.
16. Credit: Sodacan This W3C-unspecified vector image was created with Inkscape., CC BY-SA 3.0 https://creativecommons.org/licenses/by-sa/3.0 via Wikimedia Commons; https://commons.wikimedia.org/wiki/File:Tudor_Rose.svg.
17. Public Domain; https://commons.wikimedia.org/wiki/File:View_of_Henry_

VII%27s_Chapel,_Westminster_Abbey_from_Old_Palace_
Yard,_1780s.jpg.
18. Public Domain;
https://commons.wikimedia.org/wiki/File:After_Hans_Holb
ein_the_Younger_-_Portrait_of_Henry_VIII_-
_Google_Art_Project.jpg.
19. Public Domain;
https://commons.wikimedia.org/wiki/File:Anglo-
Flemish_School,_Arthur,_Prince_of_Wales_(Granard_port
rait)_-004.jpg.
20. Public Domain;
https://wikimedia.org/wiki/File:Cardinal_Thomas_Wolsey.j
pg.
21. Public Domain;
https://commons.wikimedia.org/wiki/File:Catherine_of_Ara
gon.jpg.
22. Public Domain;
https://commons.wikimedia.org/wiki/File:Daniel_Maclise_
Henry_VIIIs_first_interview_with_Anne_Boleyn.jpg.
23. Public Domain;
https://commons.wikimedia.org/wiki/File:AnneBoleynHever
.jpg.
24. Public Domain;
https://commons.wikimedia.org/wiki/File:AnneCleves.jpg.
25. Public Domain;
https://commons.wikimedia.org/wiki/File:Edward_VI_of_E
ngland_c._1546.jpg.
26. Public Domain;
https://commons.wikimedia.org/wiki/File:Queen_Catherine
_Parr_v2.jpg.
27. Public Domain;
https://commons.wikimedia.org/wiki/File:Edward_Seymour,
_Earl_of_Hertford,_Attributed_to_Hans_Eworth_(1515_-
_1574).jpg.

28. Public Domain;
https://commons.wikimedia.org/wiki/File:Lord_Grey_of_W
ilton%27s_charge_at_Pinkie.jpg.
29. Public Domain;
https://commons.wikimedia.org/wiki/File:Maria_Tudor1.jpg
.
30. Public Domain;
https://commons.wikimedia.org/wiki/File:PAUL_DELARO
CHE_-
_Ejecuci%C3%B3n_de_Lady_Jane_Grey_(National_Galler
y_de_Londres,_1834).jpg
31. Public Domain;
https://commons.wikimedia.org/wiki/File:Philip_II_portrait
_by_Titian.jpg.
32. Public Domain;
https://commons.wikimedia.org/wiki/File:Elizabeth_I_by_Ni
cholas_Hilliard.jpg.
33. Public Domain;
https://commons.wikimedia.org/wiki/File:Henry_8_with_chi
ldren.jpg.
34. Public Domain;
https://commons.wikimedia.org/wiki/File:Elizabeth_I_in_co
ronation_robes.jpg
35. Public Domain;
https://commons.wikimedia.org/wiki/File:Robert_Dudley_L
eicester.jpg.
36. Public Domain;
https://commons.wikimedia.org/wiki/File:The_Battle_of_Fl
odden.jpg.
37. Public Domain;
https://commons.wikimedia.org/wiki/File:The_Spanish_Ar
mada.jpg.
38. Credit: kitmasterbloke, CC BY 2.0
https://creativecommons.org/licenses/by/2.0 via Wikimedia

Commons;
https://commons.wikimedia.org/wiki/File:Totnes_Castle,_D
evon.jpg.
39. Public Domain;
https://commons.wikimedia.org/wiki/File:P609e_Guards_of
_the_Reign_of_Henry_VIII.jpg.
40. Credit: Nilfanion, CC BY-SA 3.0
https://creativecommons.org/licenses/by-sa/3.0 via
Wikimedia Commons;
https://commons.wikimedia.org/wiki/File:Pendennis_Castle
_keep.jpg.
41. Credit: Mary Rose Trust, CC BY-SA 3.0
https://creativecommons.org/licenses/by-sa/3.0 via
Wikimedia Commons;
https://commons.wikimedia.org/wiki/File:MaryRose-
ship_hall.jpg.
42. Credit: Metropolitan Museum of Art, CC0, via
Wikimedia Commons;
https://commons.wikimedia.org/wiki/File:Ballock_Knife_M
ET_sf26-145-7s1.jpg.
43. Public Domain;
https://commons.wikimedia.org/wiki/File:Drevnosti_RG_v3
ill130c-_Caltrop.jpg.
44. Credit: Andy Mabbett, CC BY-SA 3.0
https://creativecommons.org/licenses/by-sa/3.0 via
Wikimedia Commons;
https://commons.wikimedia.org/wiki/File:Antique_billhooks
_at_Ludlow_market.JPG
45. Credit: Ethan Doyle White, CC BY-SA 4.0
https://creativecommons.org/licenses/by-sa/4.0 via
Wikimedia Commons;
https://commons.wikimedia.org/wiki/File:Cannon_in_the_G
arden_of_Tudor_House,_Southampton.jpg.

46. Public Domain;
https://commons.wikimedia.org/wiki/File:Musket_and_Arq
uebus_Gheyn.jpg.
47. Credit: Claire H., CC BY-SA 2.0
https://creativecommons.org/licenses/by-sa/2.0 via
Wikimedia Commons;
https://commons.wikimedia.org/wiki/File:Different_Rapiers.
jpg.
48. Credit: Yale Center for British Art, CC0, via Wikimedia
Commons;
https://commons.wikimedia.org/wiki/File:Robert_Dudley_in
_Garter_Robes_ca._1587.png.
49. Public Domain;
https://commons.wikimedia.org/wiki/File:Mayor,_Alderman
,_Liveryman_1574.jpg.
50. Public Domain;
https://commons.wikimedia.org/wiki/File:Catherine_Aragon
_Henri_VIII_by_Henry_Nelson_ONeil.jpg.
51. Public Domain;
https://commons.wikimedia.org/wiki/File:Martin_Luther,_1
529.jpg.
52. Public Domain;
https://commons.wikimedia.org/wiki/File:Elizabeth_I_(Arm
ada_Portrait).jpg.
53. Credit: Ugliku, CC BY-SA 3.0
https://creativecommons.org/licenses/by-sa/3.0 via
Wikimedia Commons;
https://commons.wikimedia.org/wiki/File:Detalle_de_Hamp
ton_Court_Palace.jpg.
54. Public Domain;
https://en.wikipedia.org/wiki/File:After_Hans_Holbein_the_
Younger_-_Portrait_of_Henry_VIII_-
_Google_Art_Project.jpg.

55. Public Domain;
https://commons.wikimedia.org/wiki/File:Elizabeth_I_Rainb
ow_Portrait.jpg.

56. Credit: The Portable Antiquities Scheme/ The Trustees
of the British Museum, CC BY-SA 2.0
https://creativecommons.org/licenses/by-sa/2.0 via
Wikimedia Commons;
https://commons.wikimedia.org/wiki/File:Post-
medieval_,_Toy_(FindID_220719).jpg.

57. Credit: Beauchamp Chapel by Stephen McKay, CC BY-
SA 2.0 https://creativecommons.org/licenses/by-sa/2.0 via
Wikimedia Commons;
https://commons.wikimedia.org/wiki/File:Beauchamp_Chap
el_-_geograph.org.uk_-_2838141.jpg.

58. Unknown author, Copyrighted free use, via Wikimedia
Commons;
https://commons.wikimedia.org/wiki/File:Medieval-Jousting-
Tournaments.jpg

Printed in Great Britain
by Amazon

38526275R00136